GIVE CHRIST BACK TO US!

Give CHRIST Back to Us!

by
JUAN ARIAS

Translated by
Paul Barrett, O.F.M. Cap.

A PRIORITY EDITION

ABBEY PRESS
St. Meinrad, Indiana 47577
1975

The present work is a translation of *Cristo da riscoprire*, published by Cittadella Editrice, Assisi, Italy.

Nihil Obstat
Fr. Cuthbert McCann, O.F.M. Cap.
Censor theol. deput.

Imprimi Potest
Fr. Anthony Boran, O.F.M. Cap.
Min. Prov. Hib.

17 May 1974

Library of Congress Catalog Card Number: 75-19920
ISBN: 0-87029-051-7
Scripture quotations are from the Revised Standard Version Bible Catholic Edition, copyright © 1966 by the National Council of Churches and used by permission.
Quotation from the *Pastoral Constitution of the Church in the Modern World*, No. 19, copyright © the Daughters of St. Paul, Boston, Mass.

Printed in the U.S.A.
Abbey Press
St. Meinrad, Indiana 47577

CONTENTS

PREFACE

Of all the reactions to my book *The God I Don't Believe In,* two made a special impression on me.

The first was the opinion of a friend of mine who read the book and then remarked to me: "I read your book with pleasure and, I must confess, with more than a little curiosity. I thought it was a pity, however, that from the very first page you let it be taken for granted that you accept Christ as God. But that is exactly the thing that has tormented me for many years. In fact, I must admit that I no longer believe that He is God; and so, although your book is excellent in its own way, it is useless to me. However, I hope that it will do a lot of good for others. Indeed, if I had read it some years ago, I wouldn't have lost my faith."

The second reaction was contained in a letter that I received from a group of young people who were atheistic Marxists, but who were willing to engage in a dialogue with Christians on the basis of the dynamic revolutionary character of the Gospel. A few weeks after the publication of my book, they wrote to me saying: "We all wish to thank you for your book. We appreciate especially your 'shamelessness' in openly confessing your faith in, and love for, Christ, which, however, did not prevent you from unmasking all those caricatures of God that are current in your Church. Although we don't share your faith in Christ as God, we do confess that it is quite possible for you and us to speak together about many of the dimensions of Christ you describe, as well as about His creative, revolutionary demands on His followers, so that we can work together for man's complete liberation."

These two reactions and so many others of a similar kind, taken together with the demand of the French Communist leader, Roger Garaudy: "You clerics! Give Christ back to us!," have urged me to prepare this new book as a possible beginning for reflection by believers and non-believers, not so much on the level of ideologies but rather on the level of existentialism and of person-to-person dialogue.

In writing this book, I have had in mind especially the young people because they are the most untarnished by cultural prejudices and ideologies. And I have also kept in mind those who, although they are no longer young, have not lost heart and still believe that it is possible to make a new and authentic contribution to history.

These pages have nothing to say to, and perhaps will even irritate, those who are satisfied with their faith, those who are fully convinced that they have found the whole truth and those who are sure that they have Christ in their pockets and that there is nothing new to be discovered in Him. And unfortunately, these pages will not say anything either to those who have, for all practical purposes, shaken off their faith, not because they found it too intellectually confining but because it weighed too heavily on them and because its demands were making their life uncomfortable. These are the new bourgeois of the spirit, perhaps the only people who can really be called atheists even when they are still officially marching in the ranks of the faithful.

Although it pains me to say so, my book *The God I Don't Believe In* brought a great disappointment to these "believing atheists." When the book first appeared, people of this type eagerly reached for it with a certain morbid joy, hoping that here was a priest who would tell them that God didn't really exist and so free them from a burden that had become too uncomfortable for them.

As for the others, those who perhaps go on calling themselves atheists because they feel the pain and anger of a Christ who has been presented to them as a curb upon, and an enemy of, their need to create and their personal commitment to the construction of a world that is very different from the one we live in—well, these have not yet lost their hope of discovering in Christ "real" words that can give meaning to the new revolution that is taking place in our world.

For all these reasons, *Give Christ Back to Us!* is a new effort at facing up to some problems which many of us believe must be solved quickly if we are to make a world that is both more human and yet more divine than the one we live in. Two images of God, of the Church and of religion have extinguished in many people the hope that God still makes sense in our world, in a world which, paradoxically, while it continues to alienate and enslave men, is increasingly discovering that man is the center of history and the one who is really responsible for the continuation of creation.

The first image of the Church is that of a Church that is exclusively divine and completely unearthly, one which has forgotten or even denies the Incarnation. The second image is that of a Church that is completely angelic or satanic, a faceless Church that has no room for the deepest aspirations of man, who wants to be a God without ceasing to be a true man. That is, who wants to be like Christ, the man who is a friend of God and the God who is a friend of man.

In writing this new book I had very much in mind all those groups of young people whom I met in the past few months, the vibrant young people who believe that man alone makes history and who feel real pain because they do not yet know how to create something new, something that they themselves have made, because they still feel the weight of all the alienation that they have inherited. All of them helped me to think about their problems and to be completely honest in my search for solutions.

Let us then set out together to look for a new image of man, in the firm belief that we shall be able to find such an image.

PART ONE

Which God Has Died?

THE DEATH OF GOD IN MAN

I shall use some harsh expressions in this book; and so, before I begin, I must point out that I have spent all my fourteen years as a priest in almost unbroken contact with people who do not believe in God. During those years I have continually heard the appeal, the plea, the excuse: "I simply can't believe in a God like that!" and I have really suffered when my neighbor looked at me with pleading eyes and said: "Can you in any way agree with my atheism?"

You can easily understand then why, having spent so many years listening to people who are suffering because they cannot believe in God, I'd find it very difficult to speak about God academically and with all the airs of a pedantic professor.

Instead of dry, logical arguments, I find it much more natural to use the words of the prophets, words that may seem bitter and may sound very "argumentative." But I'd like you to glimpse through these words the tremendous love that a man has within him when, while he himself believes, he sees other men who are suffering because they can't believe even though they may want to.

There is a whole world of people who are right beside us but who are not with us, a whole world that does not believe in us or in our God. It is a relief, a kind of breathing-space, for me to be able to talk to you like this because I know that I am speaking to those who are like myself, Christians who believe as I do. Yet, even now, I cannot forget completely

3

that other world, the inhabitants of which continue to ask us, half sarcastically, but also half hopefully: "Where is your God? What possible use could He be to us?"

I have called this section of my book "The Death of God in Man" but what God has died in man? We do not accept a God whom we cannot find in man. We do not accept a God whom we cannot encounter in the deepest part of ourselves, in our own consciences. We do not accept a God whom we cannot find in love. We canot accept a God whom we are unable to find in human fellowship, in the company of our fellowmen and in brotherly love. We cannot accept a God whom we are unable to discover in the social and political dimensions of our making history along with the rest of men. And we cannot believe in a God who does not reveal himself through a Church that has a truly human face.

Let's think together about this God who cannot exist for us if we cannot find him in man. As a starting point, let's take the incident in the Gospel in which Christ is confronted by a man who has had a withered hand for many years. Christ wants to cure him, but it is the Sabbath day and the law forbids it.

But in spite of everything, Christ heals the man. If I had been present at the time, perhaps I would have asked Christ: "Why do you insist on provoking your enemies? Why do you insist on going against the law? Don't you know that this man has had his withered hand for many years? Why do you want to cure him today, the Sabbath? Why don't you wait until tomorrow? In that way you would avoid antagonizing those who believe that the law is above men. Why don't you take him to one side and tell him to wait a little, that you will cure him tomorrow and that you would thereby avoid scandal? Wouldn't it be simple prudence to wait another day? After so many years, one more day won't matter that much to him!"

But Christ does not wait until the next day, but cures the man despite the anger of those who, as the Gospel tells us, hate him and are looking for a way to get rid of him. Who is this man who is so important that Christ, just to hasten by one day the cure of his long-standing ailment, is willing to defy the law and appear as a radical and a "hothead"? Who *is* this man?

Who is my brother? At the very beginning of the human race, Cain in effect threw this question in God's face: "Who is my brother?" But this question does not belong merely to the dawn of human history; it is a question for today, for this very moment. We are always asking ourselves: "What is man?" Who is a man? Is a man worth taking any trouble over? Is it worth our while to fight for a man? Notice that I do not say to "fight for humanity," but "to fight for a man." What is a man? For many centuries we have heard it said: "Man is full of sins. Man? What is a man worth? Man is incapable of doing anything. Without God, man is nothing."

All through history we have regarded man with almost total distrust. Even we Catholics have continually been tempted to do this. In fact, I would almost go so far as to say that we have exploited original sin itself (which I do not and cannot deny because of my faith) in order to tell the whole world that man isn't worth much. And we have often used this excuse to oppose man.

What is a man? But how is it possible that, after twenty centuries of Christianity, after the Incarnation, we still go on asking: "What is a man?"; that we can still go on distrusting man, that we are afraid of man, that we are afraid of being men and of accepting fully all the consequences of the Incarnation?

As you will remember from the Bible, Adam and Eve, even if we consider them solely as figures or symbols, felt the temptation to be like God, to become God. And they tried to do so by means of magic without any personal effort. But in trying to become like God, all they did was to fail in becoming even man. They discovered that they had stopped being human because their sin consisted in not understanding that they were as God. For is not that what the Bible means to tell us when it implies that God used to walk and talk with them in the cool of the evening?

They forgot that they were like God and wanted to know evil in order to be God; that God cannot know evil and that if one wants to know evil, not only is he not God, but he is not even a man, because evil does not exist. What does exist is the man who does that evil. And at the very moment when Adam and Eve wanted to be God, they discovered that they were no longer human, they were filled with fear, felt that they were alone, were ashamed of each other and realized in a flash that they were naked. This, if you will, was symbolic: they felt alone, ashamed of themselves and no longer human.

Then they began a long history, their long, long pilgrimage in search of their humanity. But a moment arrived when God wanted man to be truly God. He wanted to free man from that homesickness that he felt in the depths of his being from the moment that God's creative hand touched his heart. Man wants to be God, and God has made it possible for man to be God. He sent His Son who became man with all the consequences, and from the moment in which God became man, man was turned into God, also with all the consequences.

But just at the moment when God offers man the possibility of being really God, and joining the family of God, of being able to sit down at God's table, of calling God Father and friend whenever he likes, because he comes from the the same race, because he can truly speak to God as a friend, because God has already entered man's world and man has entered that of God—just at that moment, man is afraid of being God. He is afraid of taking on the responsibility of accepting all the consequences of being God. He is afraid of being able to carry on the work of creation which God has confided in him, and this fear of being God drives him to leaving responsibility for everything to God the Creator, while he "chickens out." He prefers to have God go on solving his problems and to put in His hands all the responsibility and all the effort involved in making history, including that of his own life. And he does this because he is afraid of facing up to his responsibility and of accepting the wonder and the greatness which we are still incapable of receiving. In a word, he is afraid of being God. What, then, do those words of Christ to his disciples mean: "You shall do greater things than those that I have done"? It is possible to do greater things than Christ? It must be, because Christ Himself has said so (see Jn 14:12).

But if we deny this reality, this greatness of man which we have always feared, we are denying Christianity itself. We cannot accept our faith if we do not truly accept the fact that man is something immensely great, much greater than we can ever dream. Notice that I do not say "humanity," but man, man in the concrete, any single man, just because he is a man and not because he is such-and-such a man, or because he represents any particular thing, or because he has or produces something or possesses some special dignity, but merely because he is a man. For, if he is a man, he is Christ; and if he is Christ, he is God.

But why do we find it so difficult to accept that man is worth more than the whole of history? One single man, any man whatsoever, even the most debauched drunkard over whom I stumble in an alley, is more important than the whole of history, than the whole of creation, than all the money in the world? Why can't we succeed in understanding that the oldest, ugliest, most disease-ridden prostitute on the docks is immensely more important than any ideology in the world? The fact is that, although such people are depraved, they are still human; and this allows us to understand and feel the presence of Christ in them, because, as theology tells us, Christ would have died for a single man, a greatness that we find difficult to accept in man, because we have not been able to discover our own selves, because we do not accept ourselves as men, not to mention as God.

We often say that we must love others as we love ourselves. But we have not yet understood what it means to love ourselves, to accept and have confidence in ourselves, because we are too afraid of our possibilities.

We have denied the truth of the parable of the talents, because we have been afraid of the risk, because we have not fully believed that God has given us all the possibilities of creating our own history. And if I am not capable of recognizing what God has done in me by accepting the responsibility and the joy of knowing that I am Christ, with the capacity to create, to carry on the same work that God began on the first day, then it will be impossible for me to accept the true value of my neighbor.

This lack of confidence in ourselves, this pessimism, prevents us from accepting others. And therefore we always feel sad beside those who, although they have no God, still have confidence in themselves and believe more firmly than we do in the possibility that man can do something for, and even liberate, humanity. We who say that we are Christ and proclaim that we have unimaginable strength still are afraid of ourselves. We do not believe in our resources. We are incapable of imagining that we really can create more than we think we can, and since we do not have confidence in ourselves, we have none in our neighbor, in our brother, in any man whatsoever.

I need someone else if I am to discover myself, if I am to be able to know that I am a man, to understand that I am something of value, of more value than all creation. I need someone else because only in another shall I be able to discover myself. Adam needed Eve's eyes to see his own face. Have you ever thought that when we are speaking together, it is the other who sees our face and not we ourselves, and that it is we that see his face and not he? Have you ever thought of that? It seems commonplace but it contains a profound truth.

During the whole course of my day, I do not ordinarily see my own face; it is others who see it. And it is I who see the faces of others. It is I who can tell others how they look. It is I who can help others to discover what they are like, not only on the surface but what they are within themselves. And only when I look at others, when I can love others, only then can others discover what they are.

I am sure you know what I mean. How many of you have said at one time or another: "I never understood what I was until I met someone who loved me!" I begin to feel that I am a man, a person, that I am important, that I have confidence in myself and realize that I can do something in life when I meet a person who loves me and tells me that I am capable of doing something. No one can discover himself; he needs someone else to do that. But we who are locked up in our individualism, refusing to discover ourselves through our neighbor, denying the fundamental value of man, unwilling to accept the teaching of our faith that man is the center of everything, that he really is an absolute, that our whole faith revolves around man, that without man Christianity cannot exist—because of all this we have not yet come to realize that Christianity is more than a religion; it is a faith, faith in the individual man, a faith that is born of a revelation of God made man and that proclaims that man is the most important thing in our whole history.

Because we do not accept all that, we have, in practice, denied Chirst, we have denied God. And God has taken His vengeance upon us in the sense that He has had to go looking elsewhere, so that other men who do not believe in God might discover the fundamental value of man. Christ, who said one day: "They shall come from the East and the West and shall sit down in the first places," is the same Christ who said: "The publicans and harlots will go before you into the kingdom of heaven." Today, He could say: "They shall come from the East, they shall come from other places, other religions, other ideologies, and perhaps they shall be the first to understand what the Incarnation really is, what a man is." Perhaps it will be they who, in spite of having no God, will succeed in discovering man better than we ourselves did. We have taken refuge in God and have forgotten man, thus denying Christ. But they, in spite of having been left without God, in the terrible solitude of knowing that perhaps there is nothing after this life, have fixed their eyes on man, and have discovered that man is worth risking their life for. And we have to accept the humiliation of seeing that it is they who have driven us to face up to the fundamental dogma of our own faith, the Incarnation and faith in man.

We have already referred to the words of Roger Garaudy, the French Communist, those indignant words that he shouted at us: "You clerics! Give Christ back to us!" It was he, too, who said: "The Gospel still has something to say to mankind." There are many other men who haven't met God on their way through life but who have believed in man, who have made man their religion, and it is quite possible that some day they will be able to understand better than we do that Christ is also theirs.

About a year ago I was present at a small convention of writers who were also all atheists, and I was impressed, even stunned, by the great respect with which they spoke the name of Christ.

I cannot end these remarks without recalling the parable of the Last Judgment. I told you that I am constantly aware

of those who live beside us but who don't believe in our
God, yet who judge us and help us to make an examination
of conscience. Let us, then, recall the parable of the Last
Judgment, which I have read so many times, to which I
referred in my last book *The God I Don't Believe In,* and
which our ecclesiastical censors would never have passed
if it had not been spoken by Christ Himself. In this parable,
as you will remember, a multitude of men are standing in
the presence of Christ, and He says to them: "Come, O
blessed of my Father. . . , for I was hungry and you gave
me food. . . , I was in prison and you came to me there. . . ."
And they say: "We don't know what you mean! What did
we ever do for you? We did not even know you! We even
fought against you! And we wanted to know nothing about
your Church!" Yet Christ insists: "Come!" And they still
protest: "But we have never done anything for you!" And
Christ solemnly tells them: 'Everything you did for men,
you did for me." And to the others, Christ says: "Depart
from me, you cursed! I don't know any of you!" And they
cry out: "But how is it that you don't know us? Didn't
we often greet you in the market place? And how often have
we preached you!" But Christ says to them: "I do not
know you because when I was hungry, you gave me no food;
when I naked, you did not clothe me." And they exclaim:
"But what are you saying, Lord? Don't you remember the
money I gave you to buy a ciborium. . . ? And that contribution I made to build you a church? And all those times I
preached your name. . . ? And those years during which I
took part in Catholic Action. . . ? And all that I did to make
you known?" But Christ insists: "I do not know you. Get
out! because you did not help the man that was beside you,
and my religion is the religion of man. I *am* man! What
you did to the least and last of men, you did to me!"

During the Mass when the priest pronounces the words:
"This is my Body; this is my Blood," we listen in deep recol-

lection because these are the words of Christ and cannot be disregarded. But are not the words of the parable of the Last Judgment also the words of the same Christ, with the same force and truth as the words of Consecration? He Himself has said that His words will not pass away. Therefore, it is by His words that we shall be judged. And with this parable in mind, those people who are beside us, those who don't listen to us, those who do not believe, can with good reason ask us once more: "What good is that God of yours?"

GOD IS DEAD IN MAN'S CONSCIENCE

I do not know if what I have just said to you has any application to your daily life. I hope it has some such application, because, usually, when something we hear or read does not touch us personally, we have no interest in it. The man of today listens only to words that say something to him.

First of all, what about the title written above, "God is dead in man's conscience"? In what real sense can we say that God is dead in our consciences? As I said before, I cannot forget those who do not believe in us. I cannot forget all those dedicated Communists who are right now directing all their energies toward creating the Marxist paradise on earth. Nor can I forget all those who continually say to me: "What good is your Church if it does not help us to become more human, and more responsible? If it does not help us to build a world that is more just, more beautiful, more true than the one we have?"

Therefore, while I am speaking to you, I can hear the echo of the anguished words of those who do not believe in God, who do not believe in us.

God has died in our consciences to the extent that we do not know how to meet Him there, because we are afraid of our consciences, of our responsibilities, and we have preferred to exchange our consciences for anything that comes to us from outside.

Nevertheless, God must be present in the conscience of anyone who wishes to call himself a Christian. Even more, it is in conscience and in conscience alone that we can really encounter the most profound reality of our God. I am convinced that, in speaking of this matter, I am touching upon one of the most fundamental and most daring themes of our faith, one of our faith's most urgent and greatest demands. If our ideas are not sufficiently clear about what our conscience is and about the total extent of our responsibility before God, we shall never be able to regain the whole force of the Gospel, the total impact of our faith, and the Church will never be a dynamic force in our world.

I must confess that, during my years in the priesthood, I have met many Catholics who really did not know or did not understand to what extent they were responsible for their own consciences and to what extent those consciences demanded that they build their own lives and their own histories.

Many people have suffered quite a lot because they believed that they had to renounce their consciences in order to be good Catholics, in spite of the fact that the Church has never stated that she was established to replace man's conscience instead of helping and stirring it. We priests know very well from our experience in the confessional the extent to which many Catholics have forgotten what conscience really is, the extent to which they solve their problems with God, not by sharing with Him the deepest part of themselves but only from outside, from what people tell them and from what they have read.

How often does the following dialogue, or something similar, take place in the confessional?—

"I didn't go to Mass on Sunday."

"Why not?"

"I couldn't go because I have a sick baby."

"Why are you telling it in confession, then?"

"Because I was told that I had to do so."

"But what did your conscience tell you about it?"

"My conscience told me that I just couldn't go!"

"Then why are you confessing it as a sin?"

Or a young man comes into confession and says:

"I accuse myself of having kissed my fiancee."

"Do you think you committed a sin by doing that?"

"No, Father."

"Then why are you confessing it to me?"

"I was told it was a sin."

"But do you think it was a sin?"

"No, not at all!"

"Then why are you confessing it?"

We judge things from outside, but God wants us to judge them from inside. Christ Himself told us that it is not the things that enter a man, those that come from outside, which defile and stain one's conscience but rather those that are born in the heart, from within, in the conscience, such as murders, adultery, lies and all the other sins. For that very reason, Christ has told us that, if a man commits adultery in thought alone, within himself, he has committed a sin. But the truth is that ordinarily we make our examination of conscience not on the basis of a confrontation with, or assessment by, our conscience but from things outside us.

I remember that, when I was in the seminary, our examination of conscience was not a measuring of ourselves against reality but rather a review of our conduct in the light of a purely external law. We had to make our examination of conscience according to a rule of thumb that said: "I have sinned because the written regulations say that I have." Take a very simple example: I was supposed to keep silence during a certain period, but I spoke during that period. It never occurred to me to ask myself if perhaps I had spoken because my conscience urged me to help a friend, because I had to speak.

Later, I understood that, if things were like that, then

Christ would have had to make an examination of conscience in the same way and would have had to accuse Himself and regard Himself as a sinner. He would have had to make an examination of conscience something like this: "I have sinned because I defended a woman taken in adultery. I should have had her stoned, but I defended her. I did not let her be killed despite the fact that the law commanded that she be stoned. I accuse myself of having broken the Sabbath, because I cured a man on the Sabbath and it is not lawful to do so on the Sabbath. I accuse myself of having given a bad example to my apostles because one afternoon they found me speaking to a woman alone and they were put out by it."

But Christ could not have accused Himself of those things because he was acting according to His own conscience, according to His deepest convictions, which are much more important than everything that comes from outside.

What, then, is conscience for us Catholics? You won't find the word "conscience" used even once in the Gospels. For Christ "conscience" was the same as doing His Father's will. Again and again He said: "I have come to do my Father's will." But He also used to say: "He who sees me sees the Father." For Him, doing His Father's will at each moment, even when that meant going against the external law, meant being faithful to Himself, to His conscience, to His deepest convictions.

St. Paul used the word "conscience" only once and then only to refer to the capability rooted in the center of the soul, which all men, including pagans, have at their disposal. For him, conscience was a light that directed concrete actions; it was something that had authority because it was guaranteed by Christ, and because it was given to us in union with the Holy Spirit. But St. Paul's new insight consisted in what we can call "previous conscience," that is, a conscience distinct from the one which tells me that I have done good or evil *after* having done something, which is the ordinary meaning of the word "conscience." St. Paul went further than that. For St. Paul, conscience obliges by itself and includes the obligation to act, since it is the very voice of God. Not only after an action, but also before one, conscience can urge us to do something since it is God who speaks to us through that conscience. This was a new insight on the part of St. Paul which revolutionized the sphere of morality.

Conscience is man's guide in the use of his liberty. According to St. Paul, conscience can be in contrast to the law which comes from outside, since it is determined by love and beneficence. St. Paul held that there can be such a thing as an erroneous or immature conscience, but one which still obliges before God even when the action done is objectively evil, because the person with the erroneous conscience is convinced that he is doing good. To go against conscience, even when that conscience is mistaken, would be a sin, in St. Paul's eyes. A conscience that is weak, sluggish or doubtful must solve its indecision by basing itself on its own convictions, because St. Paul says that: "Whatever is not born of a personal conviction is a sin."

In Baptism, conscience has been purified, consecrated to God and bound to other men by love. (You must understand, of course, that this is not in a closely-reasoned thesis, but the teaching of St. Paul.) What Christ said especially by His actions, Paul stated plainly in words and thereby made the leap from the written law to personal conscience: "You have been called to freedom; you are free men, sons of freedom. The letter kills and conscience gives life."

In the Bible, conscience is spoken of as the heart, which is a very important point, because it unites conscience with love. According to the ancient Israelites, man is just if he follows the inclinations of his heart. But it is important to note that in the Bible, for the Semitic peoples, the heart was not merely the center of feeling, but was the whole personality of man. For a Semite, and hence for Christ, "heart" meant "personality," the depths of one's being, conscience. Therefore, when Christ proclaimed in the Beatitudes: "Blessed are the pure in heart for they shall see God," He meant that those who keep their consciences clear are blessed because they will discover God. But according to the Bible, man is tempted to have a double heart, a double conscience. Without God, he feels tempted to serve two masters at the same time. Therefore God gives him a new heart, that is, a new conscience, and writes His law in that new heart.

God writes His law in man's heart and He did so even before the coming of Christ. When God creates man He writes on his heart His fundamental law of love, which for the whole of man's life is to be the stern, profound and ultimate guide for his decisions and his responsibilities before God. Therefore St. Paul says that this law is for everyone, including pagans, because the same Creator made all men without distinction, appearing in each one of them and leaving the stamp of His fundamental love to bring them all to love. God is present in this new heart, in this conscience of man, giving it an irresistible desire for joy and happiness, and so forming it that, if he wishes to be complete, it must always be bound to goodness. Every sincere, normal, real man feels an irresistible longing for happiness welling up from the depths of his soul. I have never met a man who told me that he did not feel a vocation to joy to happiness, who did not wish to be happy, completely happy. But it is also true that, if a man is sincere, he must admit that this happiness cannot be taken apart from the profound need of his conscience to experience this happiness in conformity with goodness. And when he looks for this happiness apart from goodness, he feels that he is lacking something and that he will never be able to be really happy.

Take a very concrete example. A man may covet another man's wife, desiring her as a means of pleasure, as something that would make him happy. But at the same time, he would bring great unhappiness to her husband and her children, so that whatever happiness he might get would never be complete. He can take the other man's wife, and he may perhaps get some enjoyment from doing so, but he will never have complete, total and absolute joy. There is something within him more powerful than he, something that will always remind him that he is lacking that which would make his happiness complete. In this case, conscience has not chosen goodness equally with happiness.

Conscience is above every law, and the Christian's final decision when confronted by God is made in his own conscience. Therefore real authority, the only authority, including that of Church, springs from conscience. Only when the Church speaks to man's conscience, and only when she speaks in the name of Him who created that conscience and in terms that coincide exactly with the conscience which He created and which is present in her—only then does the Church have authority, and he who accepts this authority realizes that it is real.

But when the Church speaks in other spheres besides that of conscience, when she speaks in the name of someone else besides Him who created conscience, when she speaks in words different from those of Christ, that is, in her own name, in worldly words, then conscience may perhaps resist because it feels that the Church is not speaking to it in the name of that God who cannot contradict Himself and who is the same God present in the Church and in the depth of our souls. The Church has never denied this. She has never denied that it is man who, in final analysis, must decide according to his own conscience. For example, St. Thomas says that it is better to allow oneself to be excommunicated by the Church than to go against one's conscience; and he also says that if a person professes faith in Christ and in the Church and does not really believe what he is saying, he sins against his conscience. On the same subject, Cardinal Newman wrote that he always held that obedience to conscience, even when that conscience is erroneous, is the best way to arrive at the truth.

But no doubt you will ask me: "If that's the case, why are we so afraid of deciding according to our consciences? Why have we quit so easily? Why have we given up the idea of making history for ourselves? Why have we not been allowed on so many occasions to decide according to what we honestly felt within us when we said, often with tears in our eyes: 'But I feel that I must act like this! I feel that I cannot accept the other course!' Why have we been so often afraid to come to a decision before God, perhaps thereby going against a law that was being imposed on us from outside? Why didn't we realize that, in giving in to our fear, we were refusing to be ourselves and were abdicating our mission as men and Christians? Why have we been afraid not of the theory, since the Church has never denied the doctrine, but of actually putting this theory into practice?" Self-accusations of this type could be repeated endlessly.

One of many such accusations that have been hurled against us by those who do not believe in God is as follows: "You Christians will never be able to build anything because you are always waiting to get the answer from outside. You have no powers of creation. You will never be able to make history. You always have to wait for someone else to make up your minds. You are not capable of assuming your own responsibilities, therefore you will never be complete men." This criticism is a serious one and compels us to reflect. As Christians we should really be acting in quite the opposite way.

Since the Christian is convinced that his conscience is the voice of God, he should have greater strength and energy than others. His hope should be boundless, spurring him on to face any danger and to be afraid of nothing because he is sure that, even if his honestly-held conviction may prove to be wrong, he can never fail because Christ is with him.

Why have we insisted, too, on clinging to an external law, thereby going back to Old Testament times before the coming of Christ, for didn't Christ come to free us from the law? It was Christ who, in effect, said to us: "The law is not what saves you; I am the Saviour. I am present in you and you are my friends. You make your decisions honestly and uprightly in the light of my words and of the teaching authority of my Church when she speaks in my name, or according to the mature, considered opinion of the Christian community."

To some extent this fear is born of a very serious confusion, which nowadays we are beginning to see more clearly. We have confused the biblical concept of conscience, in which conscience is equal to God, with the Graeco-Aristotelian concept, according to which conscience is equal to reason. For the Greeks and in Aristotelian philosophy, the principle and fountain of life is the spirit. For the Christian, as for the Bible, the source of life is God, and conscience is equal to God, so that, if anything is certain and assured, it is conscience, since in it God is present in an existential and very real way.

It is difficult to see how we can go wrong. Yet our lack of confidence in conscience has led us to declare: "Beware of conscience because it can be mistaken, it can be false! Conscience must be formed!" But, if conscience is God, I cannot form it; instead, what I have to do is discover it and help everyone to discover within him the voice of God. But I cannot form conscience because I cannot form God.

God is present within me. But you may say: "What good

is the Church?" I am well aware that the dilemma is great and the tension high concerning this point, because we have not yet understood that the Church did not come to replace consciences; that Christ instituted the Church as a service, precisely in the sacred sanctuary of conscience; and that the Church helps us by preserving intact the fundamental truths that we already feel in our consciences.

And one of the truths that cannot be denied or distorted is that God is present in conscience, that man has to decide according to his own conscience, and that the Church must guarantee the continued defense of this truth lest it be falsified or corrupted. The Church and her laws must be at the service of conscience and can never legislate anything that is against the conscience of the person or a community, for then she would be going against Christ himself.

The Church, which all of us are and which is the community, helps us to mature, to advance in knowledge so that we shall not conform, saying: "Although I may be mistaken, although I may choose wrongly, I am always right with God." That won't do, it is not enough merely to have *sought* the truth. When I make a choice, besides being right with God because I chose according to my conscience, I want to be able to feel certain that I have found the truth and that I have not been mistaken.

And the whole community must similarly become mature, aided by the Holy Spirit, each part of the community maturing according to its own charism—the hierarchy, so that it may confirm that this truth is in accordance with the words of Christ, with the Christian message; and the faithful, some according to their charism of prophecy and others with the inspiration that comes to them from the Holy Spirit who works in each one of us.

When this maturing process has been accomplished and has expressed itself in a law, this law must respond perfectly with that which we feel as something fundamental

in our consciences. It is an aid and it can never be a substitute for, or an imposition upon, conscience. Today we
are gradually realizing more clearly that the laws of the
Church, too, must go on maturing, through the approval
and creativity of the whole community itself. In this way,
while remembering that the Church does a service to our
conscience, we must be quite clear that conscience is the
place where each one of us really comes face to face with
God.

Our lack of confidence in conscience has led us to fall
victims to a great fear. One of the sins of which we believers are most accused is this fear in the face of danger.
We are accused of not liking to take risks. For the same
reason, we are often told that our faith alienates us, that
instead of helping us to build our history and accomplish
something truly positive, it is a brake upon progress because we are always afraid of making a mistake, because we
are too accustomed to having our answers come to us from
outside, and because we are not capable of listening to that
profound voice of God which, as St. Paul says, obliges itself.

God urges man on from within, and man is built up from
within; otherwise, he would be formed by others, from
outside, and would never be able to be a real man. And
a Christian cannot be truly a Christian if he allows himself
be built up from outside; he must build himself up, listening to God who is within him and to his conscience through
the community which is faithful to the word of God, through
prayer and through the celebration of the Mass. Therefore
this fear of conscience is not part of the Gospel; this shy-
ing away from danger is not truly Christian.

In conclusion, I should like to recall two concrete examples from the Gospels.

We all know the parable of the talents, but there is one

very important detail in it which may have escaped our notice. The master gave each man something, five talents to one, ten to another, and one to another. Those who received five or ten talents used them; they accomplished something, and their master praised them for it. But the servant who received only one talent was afraid of losing it and, fearing his master as a severe man, went and hid it. When the master returned, he reproved the servant, condemned him and said to him: "You were afraid and didn't want to take any risks. You don't belong here because you haven't understood what it means to believe in me." We have often read this parable and regarded that servant as the model and prototype of the Christian whom Christ condemns, the over-prudent man who is always afraid of God because he knows that God is "a hard taskmaster."

But there is a detail in this parable that you may not have thought about. What about the man who, having received five or ten talents, sets about working with them and loses them, so that when his master returns, he has to tell him: "I risked your money and lost it all"? Why didn't Christ mention this type of man in His parable? Personally, I believe He did not do so because it was not necessary, since with Christ, although a man may risk his life, if he loses it he really gains it. And here we enter the profound mystery of the faith and the dynamic nature of the Church.

Then there was the example of St. Peter and his betrayal of Christ. This particular incident in the Gospel has given me, as a priest, much food for thought. Let's imagine the scene: Christ has been arrested in the Garden of Gethsemane, and at the decisive moment all the apostles had scattered in fear, as the Gospel tells us. Only Peter made a decision which, in the eyes of his terrified fellow-apostles, was imprudent and risky. He followed Christ, although at a distance, fearfully and apprehensively, because he knew that what he was doing was dangerous. But he did follow

Christ; he took a risk and ended by betraying his Master. He was the first apostate in the Church. He had made a decision according to his conscience, a decision that brought him into the gravest risk that one can run in the faith, the risk of apostasy; in Peter's case, the risk of denying Christ three times.

Whenever I read this incident in the Gospel, I always ask myself, and now I ask you: "Which was the greater sin, the fear shown by the rest of the apostles who ran away and hid so as not to commit sin, or the daring conduct of Peter who, out of love and because he could not bring himself to leave his Master all alone that night, took the risk of following Him, and ended up by betraying Him?"

My conclusion is that, if I had to choose at that moment between being one of the other apostles who, out of prudence and so as not to run the risk of betraying their Master, hid themselves far from Christ, or of being like Peter who, out of love, followed Christ even at the risk of denying Him, I would choose to take the risk that Peter took because I believe that his choice was the more Christian one and because, in the end, Christ Himself confirmed it. When the time came for our Lord to select one of the apostles to govern His Church and to strengthen his brother apostles in the faith, He chose no one but Peter. Perhaps He did this because He could read Peter's heart and understood that Peter had loved Him despite his weakness and even while he was betraying Him. Then Christ asked Peter a question: "Do you love Me more than these others?" But this was really not a question but rather a delicate means of healing the wound in Peter's heart and of saying to him: "I know very well that you love Me more than the others because you have shown Me that you do even at the risk of betraying Me."

GOD IS DEAD IN LOVE

"If we love without producing love, if by means of our lives we do not turn from being persons who love into persons who are loved, then our love is powerless." These are not the words of a saint, but of Karl Marx. If we love without producing love, our love is powerless—these could be the words of Christ and, as a man, a Christian and a priest, I can sincerely make them mine. And hence I can say that, if there is a God, then where love is powerless, where it does not produce love and where persons do not succeed in being loved, there is no God. And the young people of today, who feel the need and urgency to know that they are loved, in order to recognize and discover themselves, are saying in their own way that they want God in their love because they do not want that love to be powerless.

The Gospel tells us that he who does not love is dead, and he who does not love does not know God, that he who does not love is an atheist, the only real atheist.

In addition, we can ask ourselves if it is possible to accept the image of God which so many Christians are denying publicly in their lives, in their very love, that image of God which is offered to us by those who prevent us from loving. This is a serious and profound question. Can we accept that God who is publicly professed by those who deny love with their lives, who are afraid of love? It is true that nobody has been able to find what love is. Many people profess to know what love is and try to impose their definition of it upon others, but nobody in the whole of history has been able to give a definition of love that is acceptable to all men, just as nobody has been able to define God.

We all know that certain things are not love; we know that certain things have nothing to do with love—and I am not talking here about the free and easy associations among some classes of young people today. Instead, I am speaking, for example, about everything that is an exploitation of man in any dimension, about using God and the Church for personal aims and interests, about denying other men the right to be persons. All that has nothing to do with love.

Perhaps we shall never succeed in knowing what God is, but we certainly do know that God cannot be identified with a political philosophy, that His justice can never coincide with ours, and that, as Pope John said, perhaps even his theology does not coincide with ours. In the same way, no one can impose an image of love upon us. Not even our own faith can do this, because Christianity is not a system of morality, nor a philosophy, nor a culture, nor even a religion.

In my search for love, there is only one path from which my Christian faith forbids me to depart, the path of man. Love is inconceivable without man, just as man is inconceivable without love. A man who does not love is not a man. We have often said that he is not a Christian, but in fact he is not even a man. When we consider our western Christian civilization as a whole, we must confess that, to a great extent, God is dead in love since man no longer loves other men. Perhaps he may love God, perhaps he may love things, perhaps he may love an ideology, perhaps he may love money, but he does not love man.

The Indian poet Rabindranath Tagore has said: "The West is like a stone that has lain in a river for twenty centuries. When we pick it up, we see that outside it is clean, well polished; but when we break it, it is bone-dry inside."

The West has been submerged in the waters of Christianity for twenty centuries, but if we break open its heart, inside it is dry because it does not love man but money.

Since the Incarnation, God will always be for the Christian only a ghost and an excuse if He lacks features and a definite name. It is not enough to assert that man is Christ; we must say that Christ is man.

Have you ever thought of the fact that when Christ appeared after the Resurrection He never had his own face, His own countenance. That is precisely why no one recognized Him, not even Mary Magdalen or the disciples of Emmaus, even when they had walked several miles with Him. It certainly means that He appeared with a countenance that was not His own. And I have often asked myself if this was perhaps because, after the Resurrection, any human face was the face of Christ Himself.

What is love? You will remember that passage from St. Paul's First Epistle to the Corinthians where he tells us that even if he had faith capable of moving mountains, if he had prophetic powers and the gift of languages, and even if he gave his money to the poor, he is nothing if he does not have love. But St. Paul does not tell us what love is, for not even he knew the answer.

Love certainly is not to be equated with affluence, for if it were, God would be more present and visible in the United States or West Germany that in India or in the slums of Rio de Janeiro. But neither is it enough to become poor in order to find love. As St. Paul tells us, although I give away all my money to the poor, if I do not have love, I have nothing. Then, what is love?

Love is not to be equated with sex because, if that were so, then God would be more present in Sweden than in the Sisters who work with the lepers; He would be more present in a house of prostitution than in a man like Pope John. Love is not sex, but sex still is a holy thing, a reality and a gift fashioned by God Himself, which, far from denying, we must bless.

And here we must examine our consciences, all of us together, including the Church. It is not enough to state that young people like to do what gives them pleasure; we must listen seriously here to the young people, too, since it is they who have made us understand that we have condemned something which God Himself said was good, because everything that He has made is well made and is a source of riches for man. Sexuality is a precious power which God has made so that man can be man.

Nor is love to be equated with merrymaking and song, for then God would be more present in night clubs than in prisons, hospitals and the din of battle. But love *is* joy and happiness, and Christianity itself is a message of joy.

Love is not sacrifice, as we have been told so often, because, if it is anything, love must be creative, must beget love, as Karl Marx said. And creativity is joyful in itself; it is life, and life always produces joy. But at the same time, every joy, every creativity carries within it a certain pain, since nothing can be begotten without pain.

And the young people know all this. They know that if they want to build a love that is true and deep, if they want to get down to the most profound root of joy, they must do it at the cost of pain, and they are more aware of this than older people imagine. This is so because they know that even sexuality, that human dialogue in the flesh which God Himself has loved, is very painful and difficult even when it gives joy.

The truth is that only he who accepts the dynamic nature of life can feel free; and he suffers if even one slave remains in the world. He who wants to know if he loves must ask himself if he feels the weight of his brother's chains. I know that Christ loves me because He has set me free. I ask myself if the young people today love less than we do, if they perhaps do not feel more than we do the agony of the slavery that they see increasingly around them.

If God is love, love is God. And only where I find love do I find God. The Christian God whom we have identified with the God of love is a God who is not content with "wishing us well." From the moment we limited the dynamics of our Christian love to a simple "well-wishing," it was possible for a book to appear with the title *Love Is Not Enough,* a title which really hurt me because I feel in my bones that love must be enough, a love that can really build up a new world.

When someone says that love is not enough, he means that what we regard as love is not love at all. Christ loved us to the end and was not content with merely "wishing us well." When Peter wanted to divert Him from His path to Calvary, Christ called him "Satan"; He called Herod, who was the constituted authority, "a fox"; he called the Pharisees "vipers," and He died with the reputation of a political agitator.

Christ came to bring war and not peace, the sword and not meaningless smiles. He said that to love meant to be ready to give one's life for any man, including one's enemies. And we, with our "well-wishing," are often not capable even of collaborating with a man just because we feel an antipathy toward him or because he does not think as we do on political matters. The love of Christ seems paradoxical to us and we have tried to interpret it because in reality it brought to history a breath of true love that loves life, life that is real and not debased, that life which, to some degree, the new generations are beginning to glimpse.

When I speak about young people, I am talking about genuine ones who want to create something and not those who are dead within themselves, self-centered and drug-ridden, not only physically but also in their hearts and minds. Such as these are really old, whereas I am speaking about those who are truly young.

And when I speak about Christ's love, I mean a love that loves life, a life that meets the most profound needs of happiness, happiness for everyone and not merely for a privileged few.

Christ seems paradoxical to us. We older people have often tried to explain Christ, to translate Him, because we think that it is impossible to conceive of a Christ who says that peacemakers are blessed and then goes on to tell us that He came to bring war. A paradoxical Christ does not suit us at all, and therefore we have, as it were, trimmed Him down and adapted Him to our form of logic, a purely Aristotelian logic.

But is Christ a paradox, a contradiction? Is He, or are we? He always said "No!" to every kind of alienation, including the alienation that comes from outside, and He never accepted anything that could in any way alienate man. But we, on the contrary, do accept, even promote the alienation of man from himself, from his neighbor and from reality; and therefore we do not make history but rather anti-history.

Perhaps the only real piece of history created by humanity is that created by Christ and by those who, with Him, say "No!" to every kind of contradiction that denies man. Perhaps it is because we ourselves are in a continual state of contradiction that we think that Christ is the one who is a contradiction and a paradox.

Hence Christian love can go out to meet any other love that accepts love itself as creativity, the capacity for self-commitment, risk, madness, heroism. Christian love can make common cause with all those who love man for himself and not to please God or avoid hell; with all those who are able to come together to fight with every human means to help man become truly human, capable of making his own history, or rather, of realizing his own love.

Young people understand all this very well because they

are looking for a history that is real and programmed for everyone and not merely for the privileged classes, the new rich or tyrants; a history of love made by all, even by women, whose liberation should be undertaken since woman is still a slave and still does not have the possibility of making some of her own history, a point upon which I place great stress.

We speak about a crisis in marriage and in the family, but it is not enough to speak about such things; we must find the root cause of them. We say that the young people of today don't want to get married and that they are seeking new forms of relationships, but it is not sufficient to say that they are looking for easier forms. We must ask ourselves what woman's real position is in society, granted that we accept the family as essential to society.

If the family should be a means of liberation so that every member of it can be more human, I ask myself whether or not a woman, after marriage, succeeds in being more free, more herself, or if instead she is turned into an unpaid housemaid who doesn't even get a free afternoon each week. This is a serious problem and one which should be investigated.

Christianity does not have a monopoly of love, nor is it a new, merely spiritual form of love; it is one love among others. If it has anything new about it, this newness consists in its secret hope that love is not a flower which dies with time but one which will live forever since it is stronger than death. But it is not a different love. And here, too, the young people feel a kind of rebellion when we tell them that if they want to be Christians they must accept a love that is not really a love, a love that is disembodied, purely spiritual, one which they will never be able to understand because love is one and because they know that they must love as persons, as human beings, with all their personalities.

So, if the newness of this love consists in hope, in the fact that it is a love that does not die, our love must be more dynamic, more joyful in the struggle, more disinterested, more paradoxical, and more close-knit. But I ask myself if all this is true, or if, instead, we also find this love in those who do not carry in their hearts the hope of an immortal love. And I feel an immense respect for those who, although they do not believe that their love will continue beyond time, are yet the bravest in the fight for the liberation of their fellowmen.

For the Christian, love always has a face and a name, and he offers his life for his fellowman with whom Christ has identified himself. Offering one's life for a fellowman should not be heroism but a need and should not merit even one line in the newspapers. But if a man believes that there is no hereafter, and still offers his life for another, he should get a whole page in the newspaper; whereas for one who says that he believes that love is immortal, the offer of his life should be the most normal thing in the world.

But is that what happens, or is it quite the other way around? Only Christ has given us a sign by which we can know one another: "By this all men will know that you are my disciples, if you have love for one another" (Jn 13:35). All other identity cards or labels are useless: this is the only challenge that we can hurl—although I don't like the phrase—at the ordinary atheist, for whom offering his life would certainly be heroism.

Christianity should be less afraid of love than all other systems because faith is freedom and love liberates man. But in practice we often act as if love enchains, and this is to deny Christianity. Love is liberating, and the man who loves or who encounters love becomes free.

But perhaps it is for this very reason that we are afraid that men may love, because it is much easier to govern those who have not found freedom than to restrain free men. When a young person finds love, he becomes free and begins to be a thorn in the side of everyone else because he begins to become himself, to become a man.

Where there is no love, Satan reigns, although all the other virtues may be there, even by means of a sacrament. Where there is love, there is God, although the professional guardians of virtue may call it sin. Where there is love, there is Christianity, although the people concerned may be atheists; and where there is no love, there is no Christianity, although the crucifix and the Eucharist may be there.

And I challenge all the systems of theology to tell me that this is contrary to our faith and our Christianity, and that the true Church has ever denied this truth.

GOD IS DEAD IN THE COMMUNITY

I must begin by making a confession: I confess that I am convinced that, to a great extent, God is dead in the community because of the simple fact that the community no longer exists.

Today the community is a dream, a Utopia, something which should exist or, if you prefer, a hope for tomorrow; but today the community is no more. I have said that it is a hope, and I want to repeat that, because I should never like to have to abandon that word. The community is a hope for the future because today, as never before, we are feeling the urgency to create a different world, a world that is new, and to create it along with all our fellowmen. This urgency must be recognized. And we must acknowledge that the young, the rising generation, feel this urgency in a very special way.

This urgency may perhaps be the last cry of man's fear or else the last effort of love hidden in his soul, something which urges the new generations to try to make history together just at the moment in which the very survival of humanity is in danger. But whether it is fear or a last spark of love in man's heart, for me the important thing is that it does exist, that we are beginning to feel and live this urgency and this need to create something new, something cleaner, in union with all our fellowmen.

Hope in a different world, in a new history, one that is more our own, more shaped by each one of us, is born of that need for community which has inexplicably sprung up all of a sudden in the five continents of the world. For this urgency is not being felt only in Europe, or only in the western world, but universally.

Almost overnight, the whole of humanity has come to feel this urgency, and the new generations fully appreciate its necessity. Is it fear or love? I really don't care, because at the present day what is important is that we all feel the force of its reality.

But what is this community about which we are talking so much especially nowadays? I know very well that the word can be distasteful and even irritating to the older generation.

Sometimes I find myself asking irritably: "But what do they mean by 'community'? What is it? What good is it? Everybody should mind his own business! What are those young people always discussing! What do they hope to achieve with community?" But for the new generation, and for all those older people who have not yet surrendered the weapons of hope, it is not merely a question of a fashionable word, but one of order, a programme, a new message. Indeed, I would almost dare to say that it is their new faith.

Because of my age, I feel that I have one foot in either generation, and I think that I can understand both a little, even when my heart and my hopes are with those who do not accept human or religious isolationism as a value. I say that I think I can understand both generations because I see that history has been hard and has filled us all with disillusionment.

The first struggle against slavery brought us to the defense of the individual, a defense so energetic that it has led us to the other extreme of individualism. History shows how much we have suffered because of that individualism, and we all know very well the tribute that the Church herself had to pay to that plague of individualism: she had almost come to the point of completely betraying the true message of Christ by presenting the faith in one dimension alone.

Individualism turned out to be a disappointment. At one period, religion was afraid of self-centeredness and overstressed generosity, causing us to forget that Christ reminded us to love *ourselves* as well as others. So that on one hand there was individualism, and, on the other, fear of recognizing ourselves as having fundamental value.

We are now finally beginning to discover that it is not possible to love others if we do not love ourselves, since we cannot give something that we do not love. And if Christianity is a giving and an offering, I must offer something that I love deeply, and the greatest thing that I possess is myself. I must love myself, that wealth that God has deposited in me, that "God" which I am, in order to be able to give it to others.

Hence Christ has said that we must love others as we love ourselves. Extreme individualism made us react and caused us to go in search of the community, but in doing so we lost sight of the person and fell into collectivism. This was another drama in history, one which the older generations felt as keenly as a severe blow. They experienced the shock of losing personal values, of falling into certain types of collectivism in which the person no longer counted for anything, and they therefore rebelled by turning anew to individualism, perhaps more fiercely than before.

They retired into themselves, so that now, when confronted with the word "community," they feel bitter and say: "I have had enough of that community that doesn't allow me to be myself, that prevents me from being a person!" Until now, we must confess, the history of all attempts at forming a community have been, in practice, fiascos. But let us examine briefly, yet sincerely, the idea of community, speaking solely from the Christian point of view.

We have called the community a family, but is the family of today a community?

Among the several thousand families that I know, I doubt if there are a dozen in which the family is a real community, not only a community of love but one of persons, where something new is created continually, where each person has succeeded in truly entering into the personality of the others, where all are working together, where each member supports the others, and where each member is fully accepted. This would explain perfectly why the family is in a state of a crisis, and why the problem of divorce is so acute.

And what about the school? Is it a community? Is it one in which the children are brought together so that they can create, so that they can be exposed to the idea of creativity, so that each one can give something of his own riches to the others, so that the children can begin to express themselves, to be themselves—or is it rather a place where the children begin to learn the most rampant selfishness, where the most hateful discriminations are born, and where generosity to others is considered almost a sin?

Take a very common example: we tell a child that he shouldn't allow his friends to copy his homework because it is a sin. School is precisely the complete opposite of what a community should be, a place where each one would give to the others whatever he has. On the contrary, the school is where the children begin to learn how not to be a community and how to get the best of each other in all the professions.

And what about the religious communities? Are they communities or hotels? Or are they at times worse than hotels? At present we are at an age of profound revision, and we religious must say that we certainly haven't given a good example to you, the communities of the family, of

what a real community is. And we must confess openly that
the religious community has failed as an experiment in community. Therefore we must go in search of new ways that
are radically and profoundly different.

And what about the Church? The Church, especially,
is or ought to be essentially the prototype of the community.
Is the Church a community? Including the smallest Church,
the local Church, the parish? Is the parish a community?
Again we have to acknowledge our failure: the Church
retains no resemblance to a community.

Take a very significant example. At the very moment
when the liturgy has been reformed a little—I say a little,
because much remains to be done—along the lines of a
community, of community participation in the rites, we
have to admit that we gather together at Mass in the same
way as we do at the movies or other such places. And the
simple gesture which the liturgy asks of us, the gesture of
the kiss of peace, has made us see clearly that we are not
a community. I do not judge you, because I do not know
you, but I have been in many places and have seen that it
is still not possible to discern in this gesture of peace a
normal and spontaneous need of the community. I remember how, when the kiss of peace was first introduced in my
parish, I said plainly to the people at the appropriate moment in the liturgy: "I am now going to ask you to give
the sign of peace. I know that you are not going to do it,
but I want to see it with my own eyes and I want all of us
to confess publicly before God that we are not a community."

For if we are incapable of giving each other a handshake
or an embrace, then we who call ourselves a Christian community, the prototype of all the communities of the world,
are demonstrating the failure of the Church as a community. But this should not cause us to lose hope. A man always has the power to begin again, because he carries within him the image of God, and in spite of all disillusionment,

he always has the strength to analyze his deeds and to attempt to improve them. Today we are very well situated for committing ourselves once more to building up the community upon new foundations. We have asked ourselves why former attempts at community living failed, and we wish to reach the bottom of the question. We must go on looking, because the present concern about community is only the first sign of a springtime that has scarcely begun.

However, we want to be realistic. Yet perhaps we have already found something of value. I gave you as an example the quite ordinary and relatively unimportant instance of the kiss of peace. Nevertheless, this very difficulty that we find in our older communities does not exist among the young people. Why do the young people find the sign of peace so normal, for in communities of young people, at Youth Masses, this gesture has been received, not as something shocking, but as something spontaneous, normal and joyful. I know that a lot of older people say: "Of course, young people like to embrace each other." But that attitude is too simplistic, and the reason for the young people's spontaneous joy is deeper, and we must admit that fact.

If we analyze the matter impartially, we shall have to admit that until now we have not really discovered the value of the other person and our need of him. Only now are we beginning to build up the community once more.

We have not yet fully discovered the originality of man's nature, his unique riches, his completely original words and his singular beauty. We have regarded man as a cipher, as one among many, but not as a person who possesses his own, unique orginality that no one can change. But it will be impossible to create a real community, a community of persons, until we accept, with all its consequences, the fact that each and every man is completely and profoundly different from the rest; that one man can give me something which no other man can; that each person has something of his own to say in history and that, if he does not say it, history will thereby lack something; that each one has an originality and a wealth that the others cannot possess; that God has created us absolutely different one from the other.

It is for this reason that young people will not accept a community that makes them mere instruments, that prevents them from being themselves, that does not allow them to say what they alone know and what nobody can translate, because they have to say it themselves with their own originality, even though they know that the building up of a real community is as slow and painful as the bearing of a child. These young people of ours will never accept a community which they enter with their own originality and from which they emerge as imitations, as bad copies of someone else.

They are beginning to glimpse the fact that each of them has value as an original, an authentic work of art, and they rebel against being turned into an imitation of anyone else, because they have begun to discover or to know by intuition that no one has the right to make others over into his own image. For the Christian, God alone has the right to make others in His own image, as the Bible says, because God, since He is infinite, can make an infinite number of originals, totally different one from the other. But when a man wants to make another according to his own image and likeness, then he produces merely a bad copy and never an original work.

And we in the Church have to admit that we have sinned gravely in trying to take the place of personal conscience, to make others into our own image and likeness, to impose our spirituality as the only way of finding God, or rather one facet of the infinite God. If I try to make others into the image of my own Christianity, it may turn out to be quite non-Christian.

How many errors and mistakes we have committed, with

the best will in the world, in much of our spiritual direction!

Young people are aware of all this and they throw it in our faces; and we must have the courage to accept it. Today young people realize that the real teacher is not the one who makes disciples but the one who allows others room to become masters themselves. If the community is not creative and liberating, it will be a prison, a chain gang. But if it is creative, the peak of its creativity will consist in giving each person the possibility of realizing himself on all levels, including the level of the Church.

If we hold that the Church is creative and believe that the Holy Spirit manifests Himself through each member, we must accept the reality of this creativity in the Church and allow each person to realize himself, assisted, of course, by the Holy Spirit, but basically through his own efforts and without allowing himself to be shaped by others.

Hence the principal need of a real community is respect for others, so that the whole structure will always be at the service of the individual and not the other way around.

This point is very relevant today for the Church and for Christianity in general. If we subject men to structures and put them at the service of those structures, instead of placing the structures at the service of man, and if we are unwilling to do away with those structures when they prove hurtful to man, then we are going against Christ, because Christ said clearly and definitively that the Sabbath was made for man and not man for the Sabbath.

But to arrive at this point, we need a new faith in man, in the fact that each man is enormously richer and greater than that which he accomplishes. We must realize the need that each of us has of everyone else, even to be able to breathe.

The paradoxical thing is that, while we, in our fierce individualism, may continually declare that we are sufficient for ourselves and lock ourselves up in our own world, we do not realize that without other people we cannot even go out of our own houses or drive our cars or even breathe the air. We do not take account of others, we do not see the need that we have of so very many people who are continually at our service, enabling us to live.

Take a small example: I bring my car to the garage; I am in a hurry and I want the mechanic to fix it right away, because I need it to go on a journey. At such a time I feel the need of other people, but merely as objects, as things that are at my service and over which I have full command.

It does not occur to me to think that behind that "thing" there is a person equal to me, a man who also has a right to live, to be a person; and that he will never succeed in being a person if I am not capable of showing him and letting him see that he is necessary to me, that I cannot live without him and that his work is as important as mine.

In the same way, we come to realize the importance of garbage collectors only when they go on strike and the garbage piles up in the streets. Otherwise we never think about them. But they, too, need to feel that they are persons, to know that we understand how necessary they are for our health and well-being.

This is true not only of individual people but also of races and nations. In the world of today there are really no frontiers, for we cannot live without other nations. Today all nations have something to say to us and, above all, they feel the need of being needed.

But it is not sufficient to recognize and respect the value and originality of others. That alone does not make a community but at most a pleasant society or a group of friends. To create a real community, we must share our wealth, embrace each other, show our faith in our own personal worth and in that of others and in the belief that others can give us something of their wealth at every moment. If we are not capable of communicating deeply with each other at the personal level, we will never create a real community and we will always remain at the level of a society. And basically that is what the Church has been in practice up to now, a society—which is what we have always called it—but not a community.

The members of a society need not communicate with each other on the deepest personal level, but if I wish to create a community, I must communicate to others everything that I have which is personal, irreplaceable and unique, and I also must have the courage to do so, as well as the hope and the faith that the one with whom I am sharing has something within him that I need if I am to be fully myself.

It is not right to criticize the young people merely because they wish, in some way, to begin that profound dialogue on all levels among themselves. They are looking for something. They don't know what they have to do, due to the long history of non-communication between men, of which they see so many examples around them and even in their own families. Perhaps for years they have seen how their own fathers and mothers have not shared with each other the most intimate and deepest things within them, how their parents lived together but without really knowing each other and sharing with each other.

They've lived through all this and they don't want to go on in the same way. They want something different and, although they don't know how to find it, they go on experimenting, looking for something, some dialogue, because they realize that this is really the only thing that can create a community.

But this is very difficult to do and requires tremendous effort. I know that the older generation have given up, saying: "It is impossible for us to communicate to others something of ourselves. We simply can't do it!" They are accustomed to speaking about outside things and not about themselves and their persons, even with their spouses. But the young people of today feel that this is necessary if they are to build something like a community and then go on to create together something for history. If we do nothing more than live together, without knowing each other deeply, then it will be useless to try to do something together because it will be destroyed right away.

History proves this. Rows, divisions, hurt feelings, jealousies, and envy can all spring up where this communication at a deep level does not exist, because that is what creates real friendship, real brotherhood, which only man can achieve because only he is capable of engaging in that profound personal dialogue without which unity will never be achieved. When I read in the Gospel the words of Christ: "That they may be one so that the world may believe that you sent me," I asked myself how we can make the world believe in the coming of Christ if we cannot even appear on the surface as united, and if we are actually deeply divided on all levels, even among the clergy.

We have very little practice at communication. Nevertheless, it is the only way to create anything. When I give another something of myself, something more than words or a show of learning, or one of the masks that I usually wear, but instead speak from myself, from my person, then I create something, although it may be violent or even shocking.

The young people of today have glimpsed all of these elements that can create a new, real community, and they really want them although at times they do not succeed in achieving them. But at least they are on the way toward a community; they are looking for it, and therefore we should respect and love them. We criticize them and say that they are only following a passing fashion, that they lack mature personalities, that they are not capable of remaining alone and that therefore they want to be always in a crowd.

We say that they are heartless and self-contradictory because, on the one hand, they seem terribly selfish, even to the point of forgetting their families in order to create their own community, while, on the other hand, they seem too generous since they don't want to begin certain studies or take up certain careers because they say that they're not interested in money and that they want to study something that would be useful to other people although the salary would be less.

And we do not understand this great generosity and say that it is paradoxical, because it is completely contrary to their selfishness in forgetting their own parents. But they may be closer to the Gospel than we are, and it may be they who, with their apparent rejection of the Church, are preparing the true Church of the future for us. Christ instituted the Church as a community, one could almost say as a community of young people, in one sense a spontaneous community, a community of friends. He said this quite clearly: "I call you friends because I have told you all my secrets." And a friend is one to whom one reveals secrets. Christ revealed Himself completely to His first community and had no secrets from them: in this way He began to create His first real community whose task was to create, in turn, a new human history.

Perhaps the young people are helping us to render a little less mysterious, a little less abstract and incomprehensible, the dogma of the Trinity, which we have never been able to make them appreciate even a little and which never has moved them, a dogma which never has had anything to say to them—or perhaps even to us. Yet if I were to ask a modern teenager what did the dogma of the Trinity mean to him, he would laugh at me and say: "Not a thing! What interest could that possibly have for me?"

Because of my work, I am quite close to young people, I feel their needs, and I know that they are working toward and gradually building up something new; and I ask myself if the dogma of the Trinity, which we think is too abstract, cannot be interpreted to mean basically that our Christian God cannot be a solitary God, that He is a God who is either a community or who ceases to be God.

And it is precisely the community that, in some way, the young people are dreaming of and striving toward—a community that is so perfect, so united, that they will be able to feel that they are all really one in everything; a community in which they will all be such close friends that they will be able to tell each other everything, including their own wretchedness; a union which we have not yet come to understand, and at the same time such a great respect for the individual that nobody will dare to change him or even touch him, much less use him.

What is this God of ours, who at the same time is one God and yet three Persons completely distinct from each other, so distinct that one Person cannot be confused with the Others? Isn't the Trinity a community? Well, then, since God Himself has told us in the Bible that He created man in His own image and likeness, and since He is really One and Three, is it possible for man to be really human if he is not at the same time a community?

Isn't this perhaps what the new generation are beginning to glimpse? Is this only a passing fashion? Or is it rather a cry of the Spirit, coming from afar, from the depths of the Trinity, a cry of the Spirit that is using this insight of the younger generation to make us understand those truths of our faith which we have never succeeded in imparting to our young people and which we ourselves have always considered too abstract.

At least we should think seriously about this.

GOD IS DEAD IN POLITICS

Some of you may ask me what I mean by saying that God is dead in politics. Indeed, a friend of mine told me: "You can't talk about God being dead in politics because He was never in politics in the first place."

Obviously, God never was nor could He ever have been in politics, if we understood the term in the usual sense of something that does not really serve man and give him freedom but only uses him. Hence, unfortunately, we must say that God has never been present in what we call politics since politics has never been totally at the service of the complete and integral liberation of man.

And we must have the courage to say that today we are living in a society in which repression and the lack of true, authentic freedom is found at every hand's turn.

We are convinced that in today's world there are no political Utopias and that practically the whole of society today is oppressive and repressive. Society is sick everywhere, although in different degrees. True, some modern societies have, in some respects at least, a freedom which, unfortunately, not all of us yet possess. But it is only a difference of degree, for no country in the world can truthfully claim: "We have found complete freedom for man; we have made a society that is not oppressive; we are really at man's service, and we have given him sufficient room to be a complete man; we are free and we foster freedom."

In fact, if any country made that claim, we wouldn't believe it. And why not? Because everywhere in the world today, might makes right, instead of the other way around. The man, or the nation, that has the most power is right; whatever he says is true, and he has the power to impose his truth. When Christ told Pilate that He came into the world to bear witness to the truth, Pilate replied with a question: "What is truth?"; a question that is as alive as today's headlines. Whenever a good man speaks about truth, people look at him as if he had two heads and ask him: "But what is truth? The only truth is power!" During the reign of Fascism in Italy, it was quite usual to see written in large letters the inscription: "Mussolini is always right!" Today in the free world, such an inscription would be ridiculous, but we must have enough sincerity to confess that Fascism, in the broadest meaning of that term, has not disappeared and can take on different forms and coloration. Fascism is still alive, terrifyingly so, not only in the political sense but in the deeper sense of the deprivation of man's freedom. I would even go so far as to say that Fascism hasn't died out in the Church, because many Catholics would wholeheartedly subscribe to the inscription: "The Pope is always right! The Bishop is always right! The Parish Priest is always right! Catholicism is always right!" even in matters that are outside their province. That, too, is a form of oppression.

Yet truth cannot be identified with power or force, as we know perfectly well, and as the Church proclaims. Christ, who was the Truth, renounced power in order to give place to conscience, in order to be able to permit man to free himself. The Gospel tells us that Christ spoke as one who had authority. Why was this? Because He spoke to man's conscience. But the Church itself has, as a structure, contributed to a great extent to making society oppressive.

As one would expect, the right of might is enforced by might. But this can be done openly or behind the scenes.

Today repression is more hidden, more subtle, but more dangerous than ever before, because it disguises itself as benevolence, and many people don't recognize it for what it is. The best example of this is in the communication media, at all levels. It is dangerous for a society to think that it is free, when it is anything but free in the things that really matter. When I am confronted by a society that openly denies me some of the fundamental uses of freedom, such as the freedom of association, of expression, etc., I feel like fighting because I know that I am faced with a clear and manifest injustice. But when I can be convinced that I am free because I can vote every four years and allow other people to decide for me, and when this alone is enough to give me the illusion of freedom, then I am in great danger.

Take, for example, the myth of the welfare of the working classes and the strategy of Social Security that serves to alienate the worker and make true freedom increasingly difficult. Take party politics, which no longer serves the citizen but merely the interests of the party itself. Take the alienation that is found in the sphere of religion as a result of the shift from faith to religion, that is, from dynamic activity to passivity, from creation to submission, from confidence in man to fear of him.

The Faith is liberating, whereas certain religious forms and structures beget alienation. But we have often converted the Faith, our liberating Faith, into a religion that turns us more toward passivity than toward creativity. Here, too, the "right" of might overcomes the power of right, and the "right" of the law prevails over the right of conscience.

In society as a whole, and I repeat that there are no remaining Utopias, the person has ceased to be the center of history. A handful of individuals have taken over the right of other men to be themselves, and manipulate them at will.

The common man is no longer a person, but only a thing,

a number, an instrument to be used by those in power. To-day the world is governed by systems that have corrupted and overthrown fundamental principles of the human con-science. And this corruption is found even in what we smug-ly call the First World and the Second World. Let's be honest about it. There are no exceptions. The world is di-vided into two big groups that we can call the first and second groups. In the first group, man is worth what he possesses, and in the second, man is worth what he does and what he creates.

But only when man can fulfil himself as a dynamic, creative being will repression begin to disappear. Yet in order to be what he should be man must fulfil himself in a community in which everyone is free, since the freedom of everyone else is the manifestation of his own liberty. Only when my freedom begins at the same point as my neigh-bor's freedom, and not where his freedom ends, only then can I speak about freedom. I can begin to be free when my neighbor is, and not before.

But what are things really like today? We think that we are free and secure when we have succeeded in chaining up other people. The smaller the plot of ground that my brother owns, the wider is my freedom. But this is op-pression; there is no room here for God, the Master of free-dom, the only real Liberator.

Yet we cannot be satisfied with merely lamenting the repression of which we are all victims, and which we can see and feel. We have no taste for self-punishment, no vo-cation to be victims, and we can see no profit in a revolution or a protest that would merely be blowing off steam or would end by bringing worse repression upon us. We begin to get the idea that liberation is not easy and that giving vent to our feelings may make tomorrow less free than today. Modern youth has a capacity for thinking about tomorrow, about their successors, and they want something more creative, something more beautiful and more promising than the present. Therefore they are beginning to understand that they may fall into the trap and that it is not enough to shout: "We are in jail!" They must do something to break those chains once and for all.

Consequently, we must dig down to the roots to discover which are the real values, both personal and universal, since man is an individual and a community at the same time, as we have already seen. But if we are to get at the roots, at this final dimension; if we are to be realists and not allow ourselves to be easily taken in; if we are to make man completely free in more than one dimension, we must study the way in which man can fulfil himself, what his fundamental values are, and the order of precedence among those values.

Here I should like to present briefly five plans that are the result of an arduous search carried out by people who want to do something more than go around shouting about freedom. If we are in any way sincere and have some clear ideas, we shall recognize that this is how things ought to be.

The first thing that man must do if he is to fulfil himself is to realize, beginning with his own conscience, that he is distinct from everyone else, that he has a personal, unique value, and that he can discover this from the riches that he carries within him. The man who discovers that he is valuable, uniquely so, finds himself in due course faced with a series of questions about many things. When he is able to answer one of these questions, he is beginning to create real culture. But this one man, confronted by these questions, realizes that all around him there are other men with the same problems, who are asking themselves the same questions. Then he begins to look for answers with them, and when he finds himself joining with others to look for an answer to the fundamental problems that every man has within himself, then, if he is a man, he realizes that he needs to live with others, and that in order to live with others, he and they must organize themselves and create together something that can be an answer to his own and his neighbor's problems.

And that is where politics, real politics, begins. Men who achieve together something for their own history thereby also create something of value which, since it has been created by everyone, is at the service of everyone.

Next comes economics. When men have banded together and have produced something in all fields, they make laws to defend what they have created, as well as to defend their order of values, since true law is drawn up to defend whatever men possess and create. Then there comes into play the power of right, and not the "right" of power. If we separate power and right, or make some rights absolute in order to deny others, we fall into the common trap of reducing the person to a nameless individual, or rather we reduce the community to a faceless mass.

If I overstress the undoubted fact that I am a unique person, who must not be confused with or submitted to anyone else, and if I forget the fact that there are others besides me without whom I shall not be able to reach a full answer to my fundamental problems, then I am giving birth to the fiercest and most sterile individualism.

But if I stress only the fact that we need some political system, that we must build together, but forget the first value, which is the person, I shall fall victim to collectivism.

The society in which we live has institutionalized this collectivism, subjugating the community to the dictatorship of myths, the myths of the national state, the messianic class or the pay envelope. And in this way the whole structure has been torn down, and the actual state of affairs is completely contrary to the ideals about which I have been speaking and which we agreed should exist.

What *is* the actual state of affairs?

Today, in every part of the world, you will find society ruled by the "right" of might, by power for the sake of power, by *juridical nominalism*. There is no doubt about it: the man who has power has the "right" to impose and create his own truth. We all know, for example, what happens when the concept of private property is confused with the concept of personal property, two quite different things.

But the Church, too, has defended private property, although it is personal property that we should defend, since it is personal property and not private property that Christianity is concerned with. Private property, understood in the sense of something which its owner has the right to use or abuse, is based solely on the law of power and not on the power of law, which is at the service of man. And what happened? The confusion between private property and personal property could not last, and private property very often vanished into thin air. Consequently, private property became collective property with the serious danger, and sometimes the reality, of losing personal property, without which man cannot be man.

Then there is the *economic* system. He who has power imposes his economic system on others. He who has power determines what man shall create and how he must create it.

Next, there is the *political* system that justifies the economic system we have just mentioned; that is, politics is created to justify the economy. As I see it, there is no mystery here. It is evident that today the world is ruled, not by politics, but by economics; it is clear that it is not politics but economics that causes wars. That is so evident that there is no need even to discuss it.

Then we have the system of *ideologies* taking the place of culture and research and imposed by politics, which has been created to justify a system of economics, which in its turn was imposed by those in power. And there, in the last place, as if it were a Cinderella, with nothing to say and relegated to a private and personal corner, is poor old conscience. There you will find the most real and most vital part of man, his right to be himself, forgotten, with nobody paying any attention to it, whereas it should be in the forefront. Thus the moral initiative is left in the hands of the individual as if it were a private matter, and since the real morality is that of power, the morality of freedom is turned into a dream for idealists.

It is still enough merely to speak about a revolution? About one single revolution? As a matter of fact, we need to bring about five revolutions. That is why I ask if it is enough to speak about one revolution, which would only bind us with stronger chains. Not that I deny that we need a profound revolution which will cut to the roots, but I do think that such a revolution must take place on five planes at the same time, because if it doesn't the "right" of might will increase in strength, and men will become increasingly enslaved.

If we do not bring about these five revolutions, we shall have no hope of liberation left and we shall remain forever in the hands of a dictatorship in every sense of the word. Whether the dictatorship is red or white or some other color matters little because it will always be a dictatorship against man, and one in which God would not be present, in which He is dead. We have already spoken about the first revolution, the revolution of conscience. A person is valuable for what he is, not for what he earns or produces. Nobody can be a substitute for another person's conscience, as we have said, not even the Church. Each person must find his own vocation.

We have also said that this revolution of conscience is one of the most important, most difficult and most fearful; and therefore it is viewed as the most dangerous. But without this revolution, man will never succeed in being a man, and politics will always be the kind that we reject and for which it is certainly not worth dying.

The *second* revolution is the revolution of culture, and if we are to bring it about we must stop shrugging our shoulders and saying: "That's the way things are!" and ask instead: "Why are things like that?" The difference in attitude is enormous. If, in the face of some abuse, we simply say: "That's the way things are!" we have created nothing, and certainly not a new culture. But if we ask: "Why are things like this?" then we open the doors to creativity, to building something better.

Why do we lack a real culture? Why have we become accustomed to saying: "That's the way things are!" Has anybody got the courage to ask for the reason? Yes, but only those who have the will to free themselves and become fully creative. Take two common, even ridiculous, examples. My father has just died and I have to wear black. But I ask myself: "Why do I have to do this?" "Because that's what's done, you must wear black when your father or mother dies." And so we go on doing something that perhaps has no meaning for us. But if we sometimes stop and ask ourselves: "Why do I have to act like this?" and if many people ask themselves this question, then some new light may be thrown on a subject and we may become aware that we are right, that we must advance and find a new approach, and in this way we may create something. But if nobody has the courage to ask: "Why?" when confronted by something that comes from outside, that nobody has really examined or made his own, then we shall never have a culture.

Let's take another couple of examples, this time from the ecclesiastical point of view, one of which certainly has had far-reaching effects, while the other may or may not have had such effects. At any rate, both examples impressed me. The first is the example of Pope John, who found himself with a Church structured in such a way that he could very well have said: "That's the way things are! And having lived for eighty years with the Church, I have more reason than anyone else to say that that's the way it is. Therefore, let's go on the way we are." But instead of saying: "That's the way things are!" he asked himself: "Why?" He asked himself the same question many times and about many matters, and he reached the point when this profound "Why?" of his heart and conscience led him to say: "We must talk about it. We must get the bishops together. The whole Church must meet. We must come together, face to face, and ask ourselves why many things are the way they are and find answers to our questions."

Pope John acted like this because he was profoundly creative, because he had faith, because he was a man of deepest faith. And even those who are far from the Church have to admit that Pope John did indeed create something, that he opened the doors for a true culture of religious faith.

My second example, the effects of which are more open to discussion, concerns an archbishop who received a letter from one of the Roman Congregations telling him that an Apostolic Visitor was coming to his diocese. Now, as you know, an Apostolic Visitor is someone sent by the upper echelons of the Church to conduct an investigation about certain things that perhaps are not as they should be. The archbishop could have shrugged his shoulders and said: "That's the way things are! This is normal procedure. Every bishop may, at some time or another, receive a letter telling him about the arrival of a Visitor. And I know that this visit will be done secretly and according to the standard method. This is all quite usual." But, instead, he said: "Why?" and perhaps his question may turn out to have been creative. He said: "Why do things have to be done like this? Why must it all be so secret? Why can't it be done in some other way? Why can't I know who has accused me of something? Why am I not told the reason behind this visitation? Why do I have to just sit and say nothing?" All these whys were honest questions that in no way did violence to his conscience. And actually, things did turn out differently. It may well be that this incident helped the church to revise a precedure that had been accepted hitherto because everybody merely said: "That's the way things are."

Until somebody has the courage to ask: "Why is this so?" new opportunities for creating better things will not arise. And the Christian who believes in the God within him and the dynamic nature of his faith must always believe in the possibility of creating something better. We must once more find true culture, that culture which is etymologically related to the cultivation of the earth. We have prostituted culture by transforming it into ideology, whereas true culture begins for man with his contact with the earth. And here it is necessary that we feel a great respect for the function which farmers still have to perform. We often speak about the great common sense of farmers, and so it is reasonable that we should start our search for culture from the solid foundation of the land.

Perhaps it was not mere chance that Pope John who was possibly the greatest and certainly the most beloved of modern Pontiffs, came from farming stock. We must get away from the culture of the technocrats, as well as from the culture of those who are intent on making bigger and better mousetraps. The call of culture to get back to the land is urgent, for to lose the sense of the land, to reject agriculture in favor of technology would be to renounce real human culture. As we now know to our cost, the law of technology is ruthless; it has poisoned the land, the rivers, the air and the sea; and we are losing those fundamental values that permit us to be men. We are losing the purity of the very products of the soil, of all the things that go to make up creation. We are prostituting creation itself.

A time will come when men will no longer be able to be men, when the earth, from which they sprang, will cease to be earth, when the air will cease to be air, the water to be water; when bread will cease to be bread.

And this is very important and urgent if man is to be able to fulfil himself, if he is to be able even to talk about politics. Otherwise, we shall become mere phenomena, monsters, faceless things; and then it will be useless to speak about politics because it will be useless to speak about men.

This culture which begins with the land must regain the fundamental values of language itself in the enormous Babel of today's world, in which words no longer mean what they should mean according to their roots. When I speak about freedom, I ask myself what does freedom mean today. This one word "freedom" can have two completely opposite meanings when used by two different people. This one word is the war-cry of those who know what it means to be free, and also of those who mean to enslave their fellowmen. And what about the word "conscience"? The same thing holds for it; it, too, has been used as a mere instrument. No longer do fundamental words mean all that they ought to mean, and so there is no way for people to understand each other; we are living in a real Babel.

In speaking about the call of the land perhaps we shall have to recognize that it is the farm people who have kept the purest and most genuine meaning of the word "conscience." When a man from the country says that he is acting according to his conscience, he means exactly the same as the Bible, referring to that honesty with oneself of which we have spoken. Perhaps it is not by chance that it is a country child who figures in the old joke that mathematics teachers used to tell, "If your father bought a cow for $100 and then sold it for $500, what would he have earned?" And the child answers: "A couple of years in jail!" "Why?" "Because he'd be a thief!"

That is the real meaning of conscience. And we would have to conduct a widespread investigation in order to recover the basic meaning of those simple words which, when we heard them from our mothers, still meant something, but which were later debased by a thousand dark intrigues.

The *third* revolution is that of politics itself, in its most concrete sense, that is, going from party politics to the politics of unity, of the community, of human aims, where liberty does not consist in eliminating the freedom of others in order to enlarge one's own, but where one's personal freedom is equal to the freedom of everyone else.

And here I think we have no alternative but to attain—and I'd like you to understand what I am about to say in the most profound sense of man's fulfilment—to attain what can be called a directive democracy, a true democracy, not as an ideology but as the possibility that every man has of making his own history, of attaining everything that he can and ought to attain.

We must start from this possibility that each man ought to have of fulfilling his own history, not delegating it to others, but attaining it by himself to the greatest possible degree. And if we do not so begin we shall never attain real politics but shall be formed by other people and shall never be ourselves. It is true that a maturing process is necessary to reach this end. We are still very far from it, but it is possible to reach it. In fact, it is the only possible way of being able to create a politics of men, a politics of which we see so many repellent extremes today.

Take the workers, for example. I don't know whether or not they realize that they haven't even got the possibility of carrying on their own struggle, of pressing their claims, since that is all imposed on them by others. For example, when someone higher up decides that a strike would be good strategy—and I don't deny that possibility but have always supported it—the workers accept the idea and go out on strike, without adverting to the fact that they haven't a chance of carrying the struggle to a finish and that even the method of struggle is imposed on them. But instead of going on strike, they could say: "We want to do things in a different way, because this method may perhaps work against us." In many cases, that's the way they feel, but they haven't got the least chance of carrying out the struggle on their own.

That is just one example, but we could give many others. If we are not able to get away from these outmoded strategies which sprang from decadent philosophies that take it for granted that only a few privileged people are capable of thinking for everyone else, of drawing up programmes for them, and that the common herd must leave everything in their hands, then we shall never create a politics in which there is room for God, since it is the whole man who must be fulfilled, and since every man ought to be the maker of his own history, with the possibility of achieving everything that he is capable of doing.

The *fourth* revolution must take place in the sphere of work and economics. The development of economics consists in having the initiative pass from capital to labor. In this way, the ordinary people will have the possibility of knowing that their work does not serve for the enrichment of a few but that, besides giving them a just recompense, it will be work carried out in common. In this case, it is evident that everyone must take part in drawing up the programme. Take a very ordinary example. In any fairly large city at Christmas time, the city center, where fewest people live, is lighted up and decorated at great cost. The shopping centers, where practically nobody lives, are made the most beautiful and are the best-lighted streets in the city, while in the working class districts and the slums, the home of the workers who are really making history, there are no decorations, bad street lighting or none at all. The people here don't have the time to go downtown and enjoy the lights, and they may even lack the necessities of life. Obviously, if the majority of the people had anything to say about the city government, things would be quite different.

One of the greatest revolutions must be brought about in the area of work because, since man is creative and fulfils himself through his work, we must condemn the false philosophy or pseudo-theology of "free time"; we must have a great, radical revolution. But what do I mean by "free time"? If I accept the fact that "free time" exists, I also accept the fact that the time spent in work is a time of slavery. And this would be the greatest insult to, and the most profound rejection of, society, because if man is a slave and not free when he is working, if he is free only after his work, he has failed completely.

The reason for this is obvious. In practice, most men spend their whole day working, so that, if a man is a slave during the time he is working, obviously he will never be able to free himself. His work will not help him to be a man, to be free; and it is only through his work that he can succeed in being both. Hence it is easy to see why man will never succeed in being a man. Yet we easily accept the idea of "free time," in which man may fulfil himself to a certain degree, and thereby we prove that work is a time of slavery.

You can see, then, that the revolution which must be brought about is immense. I'd like to emphasize something that is very important to me from the Christian point of view. To solve this problem of work, we've often said in the past: "The important thing is to sanctify our work," and at present there are some very powerful associations which follow this spirituality. But if I accept the principle that work, as it is done today, is a time of slavery, I cannot believe that I can sanctify something that enslaves me. I must bring about a revolution and strive to overthrow that whole system of work, because I cannot sanctify something that goes against man and prevents him from fulfilling himself.

To say that I must sanctify my work, as it is organized at present, is to say that God agrees with the present system; this would be to deny God and say that He is dead in work. On the contrary, it is necessary to do everything possible to bring out the fact that work in the modern world enslaves man, does not allow him to be himself, and does not let him be creative; that man is increasingly becoming a machine, more of a slave and less a free man, less capable of carrying out his true vocation.

Finally, there must be a *fifth* revolution, in the juridical sphere. Until now, the State has been the boss and the citizen the slave. But now the human person must become the universal legislator, while the State must be only an instrument for maintaining due order in society. Here, too, if we give first place to that which ought to be at the service of men, we are destroying his rights. The law is not yet at the service of all men to defend their fundamental values, but is used in such a way that, not only is man not free, but he can never succeed in liberating himself. If our system of law is not reorganized, obviously we shall never have the possibility of being free or of believing in such a liberating law.

This whole idea may seem Utopian, but do we have any alternative? Should we be resigned to being slaves? Or should we rise up and start a revolution which, in the long run, will enslave us still more? I do not think that it is Utopian, because as we have already said, man, and his conscience, is stronger than the structures that are crowding in to enslave him. We have seen how, down through the centuries, no structure has been able to crush man once and for all: man, and his conscience, is stronger than structures.

And there are always men who succeed in finding an answer to their questions, and in becoming aware of their lack of freedom.

Man can do it. If one man has succeeded in doing something, that's enough to show that it is possible for others. And if three men have been able to join together to achieve something that is true and real, then the whole of humanity can do it too.

To say that this is Utopian, that it is difficult, is to say that we don't believe in God; it is to say that God does not have a place in politics; it is to accept the death of God in the building up of the human community.

GOD IS DEAD IN THE CHURCH

In this section I am going to speak about things that affect me in a very special way as a man, as a Christian and as a priest; about things that I love and in which I believe deeply, things that hurt and wound me. I cannot forget those who go on asking me: "What good is your Church?" and especially those who are sincerely seeking the truth, those whom we have abandoned, those who could understand and accept truths from us but who do not succeed, through our fault.

I know quite well that there are many of you who do not think as I do because you have not been in contact with or felt the pain of those who do not believe because of us. You will not be able to understand what I'm saying, what I'm complaining about, although my complaints are really inspired by love, but by a love that is painful to me, especially when I speak about the death of God in the Church.

Which God has died in the Church? Why are there so many people who say to us: "Christ, yes! The Church, no! The Gospel, yes! Christianity, no!" Why is there still so much truth in the words of the Indian poet: "Christ, if your followers were like you, today India would be yours"?

These are very serious questions, and they are directed at each one of us. Today more than ever, every time I mention the Church, I have to emphasize the fact that we are all involved, from the Pope down to the least of the faithful; that today we cannot be Pharisees; that we cannot say that this holds good only for the Pope, or for the bishop, or for the parish priest, or for Catholic Action, etc. We are all involved when we speak about the Church, about the death of God in the Church.

We must affirm that Christ is the Church, but we cannot always say that the Church is Christ. When I say that Christ is the Church, I mean that I can and ought to find in the Church everything that I find in Christ, but at the same time I say that I cannot accept as the Church whatever I do not find in Christ. But if we go on declaring that the Church is Christ, we will run the risk of attributing to Christ all our miseries, scandals and sins. And then people will say: "This Church is not Christ. This Church is no use to us because it is full of human weakness."

Faced with a world that is becoming deeply atheistic, that says it no longer believes in God or in the Church, it is useless for us merely to bemoan the fact or to content ourselves with saying that there is no longer any faith in the world. The Church herself, meeting in solemn Council, has said that a large part of this lamentable situation is due to us.

Here are the very words of the Council, taken from the *Pastoral Constitution of the Church in the Modern World,* No. 19:

> Hence believers can have more than a little to do with the birth of atheism. To the extent that they neglect their own training in the faith, or teach erroneous doctrine, or are deficient in their religious, moral or social life, they must be said to conceal rather than reveal the authentic face of God and religion.

Consequently, by preaching the Gospel badly or because of a theology that is not the theology of Christ and our faith, or because we have been deficient in our religious, moral, or social life, we have concealed rather than revealed the authentic face of God and religion. If someone had used these words before the time of the Council, no doubt a lot of people would have accused him of being a trouble-maker.

Accordingly, we must ask ourselves and not someone else, since we are the Church, what we must do to make the face of God visible once more, seeing that we have hidden it. And we can ask an even more searching question, namely, why present-day atheism and the problem of the death of God have arisen precisely in the heart of our Christian civilization; why has this weed sprung up in the Christian garden; why has atheism begun and why does it continue to flourish in the midst of Christianity?

Is it possible that those words of the Vatican Council were true even of the first centuries of Christianity? Is it possible that the greater part of the concrete reality of Christ still has to be revealed? For Christ has been transmitted to us by means of cultures and historical realities that were in direct contradiction to Christ Himself. Christ came to bring something new to earth, to start a real revolution, to free man once and for all, and permit him to be truly man and to create a new history, made by him and not imposed on him by others, a history forged by the full power of man's imagination. Christ came to give us not only that possibility but also the power of invention, of going against a stream of anti-history. But was Christ betrayed, to a great extent, by His first followers? They were the first to feel the temptation to exchange the face of Christ for that of a decadent history, made by men for whom history took no account of the oppressed, the common people, the silent masses, those who could not speak for themselves.

Thus, from the very beginning, Christ was passed on to us through a culture that had already been formed, through historical realities that were opposed to man himself.

And this continued for centuries. The temptation was strong, admittedly, but we must not be afraid to confess it.

I am not afraid to do so, precisely because I believe in the Church; because I believe that the Holy Spirit is in the Church; because I know that the Church can never be destroyed despite everything we may do against her; because conscience is stronger than all the structures, I know quite well that the Spirit, who is in each person, is stronger than the Church, than all our sins and weaknesses.

I know this perfectly well. Even St. Peter had the temptation to mix Christ, His revolution and His faith, with Hebraism. He wanted to reconcile both elements, telling his Christian converts that they were still Jews and should observe the Mosaic Law. It was this that led St. Paul to oppose St. Peter "to the face." Thus began the first tragedy in the history of our faith.

And so it continued for centuries. There is no reason to hide it; it is a fact of history; but it is also one of our sins, and the Church herself tells us so. It is a sin that we commit every time we exchange the Gospel for the world's culture, every time that, instead of showing the face of Christ, we reveal the face of a history that is really anti-history. We have said that God is dead wherever man cannot be a man, wherever he is not accepted as a man; that God is dead where conscience is replaced by any authority, from above or from outside; where conscience is not recognized as the voice of God within ourselves, as the Gospel tells us. We have said that we cannot find God where there is not a love that is creative, revolutionary, a love that is sacrifice, a love which led Christ to die for us. As we have said, we cannot find God where men are not able to come together to build history as a community and not as single individuals.

We have said too that there can be no place for God where politics does not permit men to create history together, by themselves, where history is imposed from above by a privileged class. And today we say that God is dead because He can exist only in a Church which has a human face; in a Church which, as Christ said quite clearly, is not of this world: "My kingdom is not of this world."

Hence, whenever the Church feels the temptation to organize herself and present herself as a kingdom of this world, we deny her. Christ disappears from her and goes on working elsewhere, because there is no Church there. Therefore, we cannot recognize a Church that is made in that fashion.

But what do we mean when we say that the kingdom of Christ is not of this world? We mean that the kingdom of God must be something so different that it is worth our while to accept faith in it, so different and so new that we can discover God's presence in that Church, in that community. But when we lack this faith, when we believe that there is no possibility of building the Church unless we do so in the image of this world—and that has been the continual temptation for the Church down through the centuries —then we deny the very origin and power of the Church.

A kingdom that belongs to this world cannot be sustained without certain historical categories.

A kingdom of this world cannot be upheld without power; it cannot be maintained without economic power, without defenses, without politics, without diplomacy, without some people imposing on others, without some class warfare, and without so many things which are necessary if the kingdom is not to be overthrown.

But the Church is different. The Church's power is her weakness, and she does not need any of those things we've mentioned to live and persist. On the contrary, the Church must show the world that God is present in her because she can live without any of those things; that she can go on living and speaking to men without outside help: that she is a Church, a community that is capable of maintaining itself without any of those structures; one that has found its own way of governing itself; a Church, a community that can show that men can live as brothers and can make history together; a Church that shows that, while preserving the greatest respect for the conscience of each man, it is possible to create something new; a Church that shows that she can support herself without money, that she has no need of economic power, human diplomacy, or oppression; that she can allow men to be free; that she is not afraid of love, or of those who fight against her, or of being persecuted, because she knows that in her heart there is a force that is new, different and more powerful than all those things which are necessary for a kingdom of this world to exist and stand.

It was only when the Church appeared before the world like this that even those who had not hitherto accepted her had to surrender and say: "There is something here that we cannot understand." In the first centuries of Christianity, there were the Christians, who were able to love their enemies and resist every form of oppression, even to the extent of giving up their lives. And there were the others who said: "What kind of people are these? What's the matter with them? Are they holy—or just plain crazy?" Only when those who do not know or believe in us begin to say: "Who are these people? Are they crazy, or are they holy?"; only then shall we be sure that Christ is becoming visible.

But when we present ourselves and even feel happy and proud to appear before the world as a power, with all the things that the world, too, likes to display, then certainly Christ cannot be made visible. We cannot enter into competition with the world, since our strength is quite different.

This is precisely why many people, when they do not see the real face of the Church, say: "Of what use is it to us?" But when some member of the Church, and one is enough, presents this real face to the world, then he can really shake the world to its foundations, so that even those who do not believe are forced to remark: "This fellow really has got something!"

Take Pope John, for example. How did he succeed in stirring even the most unlikely people so deeply? I remember a long conversation that I had with a worker. Having attacked the Church, he took out his wallet and showed me a picture of Pope John, saying: "But I'm all for him!" And why this enthusiasm for Pope John? Because he was a man. The Church must have a human face, because our God became man and appeared on earth without worldly influence. He came as a man who made strength out of His weakness and who said: "In my kingdom the greatest are the least, and all will be equal. The greatest will have to serve the rest. In my kingdom, he who is not with me is against me." How many times did He have to say to the Apostles: "You still don't understand. My kingdom is different"?

And if Christ were to come today, He would tell all of us, from the Pope to the least of the faithful: "You still haven't understood, because there are so many people who cannot see my face, with its joy and its hope, for which man is waiting and for which he has been yearning in the depths of his heart for so long. And they haven't succeeded in seeing my face because you still understand nothing, and you haven't even begun to understand." Pope John said that we have scarcely yet begun to understand the Gospel. But this does not mean that the Holy Spirit has taken a vacation; it does not mean that He has stopped working or that Christ sits idly by. The Church is still very much alive. What happens is that, paradoxically, mysteriously and incredibly, He has gone on creating His Church and seeking out the most important elements of the Church, even outside our walls. Today we are confronted with a great paradox that gives us food for thought and ought to make us tremble, but which, at the same time, gives us hope. This is the paradox of seeing that many modern atheists, who, we are convinced, reject God completely, are in a sense nearer the Gospel than are we who make up the Christian Church of history.

The Church is renewing herself and examining her conscience. The Church of the Council says: "That is not our Church." And why not? Because the world of atheism is full of sincere men, of men who have searched earnestly, who cannot accept that God whom we cannot accept either, who cannot accept the face of the Church which we cannot accept either. Men like these have travelled a long road of suffering and, when they found themselves without God and without a Church, they looked to man to give them a minimum of hope, digging down to his deepest roots; and, paradoxically, they have discovered man more truly than we have. But, by discovering man, they have met Christ, although they may not know it yet, and may not be able to admit it. They have found the fundamental dogma of our faith, one which we had forgotten because it was the most difficult to accept. And we have taken refuge in a God whom we could not see, who did not weep, or beg for bread, who could not cry out to us because He was nailed to a cross. In contrast, the atheists have taken refuge in man and have seen him weeping, in chains, and have cried out: "No!" to many of the ways in which man has been used. They have set out to defend man, but in doing so they are actually defending the dogma of the Incarnation, which is the central dogma of our faith.

Hence the time has come to ask ourselves: "Who is the believer, and who the unbeliever?" Considering the great multitude of people who say "No!" to the Church, but "Yes" to the Gospel, who say "No!" to Christians, but "Yes!" to Christ, isn't it likely that what Pope Pius XII foretold will come true, namely, that the day will arrive when those who say that they don't believe will come into our Church, while perhaps many of those in the Church will leave?

This paradox is also a great hope for those who believe that, as the Communist, Roger Garaudy, has remarked, Christ "still has something to say"; it is a hope for those who are looking for man's true liberation, and for those who want and love a Church that is different from the one they have seen, so frequently full of weaknesses and sins, and not bearing the face of man much less of God.

As for all those who suffer, who are searching, who say with Joan of Arc: "But how is it possible that I should not be in the Church when I want to be in it?", I am convinced that they will soon be the new Christians and will say to us new words, taken from a Gospel which we ignored, through laziness, or evasion, or because we took refuge in a God whom we could not see weeping, words that we have not had the courage to read. Perhaps they will tell us new things about the Gospel.

I shall always remember the Gospel lesson that I got from the life of a man who had been a Communist, who had spent twenty years in prison and was blind as the result of torture. When he found Christ and the Gospel, he made us see in one lesson an image of Christ that I had never seen before, and that I, although a priest, had not even dreamed possible. This blind man, after twenty years of torture, having denied the Church and Christ, was able to reveal to us the full riches of certain pages of the Gospel, making us tremble as we listened to him.

In him I met a new Christian, the symbol of a generation that is arising. For that reason, I have hope in the young people who, in their own harsh and vehement way, speak about destroying the Church and declare: "We don't like structures!" They want something else, something different. They don't know how to express themselves, but I believe that, in their hearts, they are saying: "No!" to a God which the Church herself, the real Church, rejects.

And this is our true hope, because they want something that is more genuine, more true, something that is of use to them in creating a new history, one that is clean, made by everyone and that has the real face of Christ. For these young people do not reject Christ, since they say: "Christ, yes! You people, no!"

I would like to leave this question like a knife plunged into your hearts. Yet I don't want to stop at mere words but wish that you would all think deeply, because every time someone says to us Christians: "Christ, yes! You people, no!" we must at least conclude that there is something in us that is not of Christ; that God has died in some way in us; that we have the obligation to revive Him, to fight so that our God may be presented as the real God and not as a God who does not exist, as one whom we cannot accept.

Only in this way will the Church still be able to say anything to those who are looking for hope. Only in this way will they not have to go looking for that hope in other leaders who, even though they may be sincere, even with all the strength of their goodwill, will never have the real words of eternal life that Christ, our Christ, has. If we do not believe that it was Christ who said the true, definitive word which created history; that the only true history is that which corresponds with His words; that only when He says: "Freedom" is freedom created; that only when He pronounces the word "love" is love reborn; and that only when He believes in man can man be man—if we do not believe this, then we should not pass ourselves off as Christians.

I'd like to end by repeating some words I wrote about the Church I love, words I would like you to think about because I am convinced that you want and love the same Church as I, because, basically, I have only tried to say aloud what I'm sure most of you already feel.

If we are united on this point, it means that we are all moved by the same spirit that cries out from the depths of our hearts the same word and the same hope, and that shows us the same face of a Church which still has something to say to us so that we may be ourselves, so that we may be men and can live as brothers, so that war may disappear once and for all, and love may once more regain its proper place among us.

The Church that I love is:
The one who is more afraid of those who do not move in order that they may not sin than of those who have sinned because they are trying to advance;
The one who speaks to me more about God than about the devil, more about heaven than about hell, more about beauty than about sin, more about freedom than about obedience, more about hope than about authority, more about love than about immorality, more about Christ than about herself, more about the world than about the angels, more about the hunger of the poor than about collaboration with the rich, more about good than about bad, more about what is permitted to me than about what is forbidden to me, more about what is still open to enquiry than about what has already been solved, more about today than about yesterday;
The one who not only does not fear those who open up new paths but even encourages and protects them;
The one who prefers to defend saints while they are alive rather than when they are dead;
The one who does not turn up her nose at anything new before having even tried it. . . ;
The one who is conscious of being able to distribute God in Holy Communion and yet of being in constant need of everybody. . . ;
The one who is more concerned about being authentic than about being big; more concerned about being sim-

*ple and open to light than about being powerful; more
worried about being ecumenical than about being dogmatic; more desirous of being holy than of being popu-
lar; more eager to belong to everybody than to be mono-
lithic. . . ;*

*The one who is more a mother than a queen, more an
advocate than a judge, more a teacher than a policeman;
The one whose message, essence, word, life and mission
is: "Yes!", "Let it be done!", "Arise and walk!", "Go!",
"Search!", Cast out the nets once more!"; instead of
"No!", "Wait!", "Go back!", "Renounce!", "That's
enough!";*

*The one who always has the fire lighted for all those who
are cold and lonely; the bread newly baked for all those
who are hungry; and the door open, the lamp lighted
and the bed made for all those who walk the road, tired,
in search of a truth and a love that they have not yet
found.*

(The God I Don't Believe In, pp. 97-102.)

I don't want to finish without mentioning a name which,
although I haven't used it yet, was in my mind and heart
every time I spoke to you about Christ or about true Christians. I thought about this name because I don't want everything I've said to remain on the level of mere words. All
the self-criticism that we have sincerely and unashamedly
voiced to those who don't believe in us would be only bla-
tant hypocrisy if we were not really committed to it in love.

The name to which I am referring is that of Mary, Mother of Christ, the purest example of total self-sacrifice. At
the wedding feast of Cana, Mary asked Christ for a miracle.
Christ replied that His time had not yet come, but Mary
still wanted the miracle, although, as we know, to anticipate Christ's hour meant to anticipate the cross and lose
her Son that much sooner. On that occasion, Mary loved
us more than herself; and she was able to sacrifice her Son

so that we might live on after He had gone to the Father. She remained for twenty years in the heart of the first Christian community to remind it continually of her Son's message of hope, to recall to the apostles that the community is a living reality, to help them remain united, not to be afraid, and to give their lives for their fellowmen, so that they would make the image of her Son visible to all mankind. For Mary, those twenty years were years of suffering and hope, without the visible presence of her Son.

Mary is still present today, with Christ, in our history, a fact which we cannot forget when we speak about Christianity and about hope. And when we feel ourselves invaded by fear from outside, even though we go on hoping in our hearts, we need words of consolation and hope, the words of a mother and a Christian who knows what it means to love because she knows what it means to sacrifice herself completely. And we need her help because we are engaged in a struggle that is by no means easy, in a revolution that will inevitably bring us pain, and in a commitment that is very demanding.

Mary is the example of the committed Christian, for she believed joyfully and with all her heart that her Son was not dead and that, consequently, love and hope were not dead either.

A Christ Who is Always New

VIRTUE IS NOT A COMPROMISE

According to the old saying, virtue lies in the middle ground between two extremes. But is the proverb right?

It certainly doesn't fit Christ, because He was a radical: "He who is not with me is against me"; "You cannot serve God and mammon"; "I came to cast fire upon the earth; and would that it were already kindled!"

Christ was on the side of the poor and the enslaved: "I have come to preach good news to the poor and to save that which was lost." Christ was a revolutionary: "He stirs up the people."

Christ never accepted half-truths or used diplomatic evasions, and they accused Him of being "a blasphemer."

If Christ had not been God, He would have passed into history as a "fanatical prophet" who spoke in paradoxes and contradictions, blessing the peacemakers and saying that He had come to separate the son from the father; cursing the rich and yet eating with them; curing illness and relieving pain, yet dying on a cross alone; speaking in parables "so that they may not understand"; provoking the Jews by telling them that He would rebuild the Temple in three days.

Christ never appears as a political conciliator. He is always on the side of something or someone; on the side of the Publican against the Pharisee; on the side of the woman taken in adultery against her hypocritical accusers; on the side of the children against the Apostles' ill-temper; on the side of Magdalen against Simon the Pharisee.

He argued heatedly with His adversaries and passionately defended the weak and the downtrodden.

It is curious to see that He was accused of being possessed by a devil.

A Christ who is "meek and mild," agreeing with everyone and going along with everything, is certainly not the Christ of the Gospel who, in all probability, has been understood only by the great saints or the great sinners.

Mary, unstained by sin, and Peter, the apostate, were the most disconcerted by certain attitudes of Christ, but they were also the ones who entered most deeply into the mystery of His life.

Like so many such sayings, the adage that virtue is in the middle between extremes is more anti-Gospel that truthful. And the origin or the application of this slogan has all the appearances of an attempt to justify our cowardice in being unwilling to adopt radical attitudes.

We have transferred the standards of human diplomacy to the teachings of the Gospel, which are true even though they may lead to crucifixion.

If virtue really lay in the middle ground, Christ would not have been virtuous, nor would the prophets or the great saints of history.

Can anyone say that St. Francis of Assisi placed his virtue of poverty "in the middle"?

The saints never engaged in or accepted political or diplomatic balancing-acts. Like Christ they loved without measure, giving all that they had and abandoning themselves to the irresistible force of the Spirit who blows "where He wills" and not where it is convenient.

God is generous; His measure for everything is superabundance. Should, then, our response to His generosity be a measured one?

His place is always out ahead, breaking the trail, and His

method of teaching is to take by surprise and to condemn idols.

For God, sin consists in standing still, because love is always on the move, always creating, tirelessly seeking.

In God, there is no such thing as enough: "You shall see greater things than these"; "Whatever you bind on earth shall be bound in heaven, and whatever you loose on earth shall be loosed in heaven." God always forgives because, in Him, there are no boundaries.

With God, making mistakes and falling are not the important things, but rather the will to walk beside Him and along His paths.

In God, there are no "city centers," no market places, but only roads that lead to the Infinite, which is He.

Our classical idea of prudence places virtue in the middle ground, in a nice balance between extremes; but if this were true, there would be no place for heroic virtue, which is always excessive in the context of middle-class virtue.

It is curious to reflect that prudence is one of the great virtues which the Church requires for canonization, and this is causing great concern to promoters of Pope John XXIII's cause. Actually, all the saints were "imprudent" and denied by their actions that virtue really lies in the middle ground. Indeed, for them virtue always lay in the extremes.

The usual way to get out of this dilemma is to blame it all on the Holy Spirit by saying that He inspired the Saints to do many things which are "to be admired but not imitated."

But in that case, is it not reasonable to conclude that, for the Holy Spirit, virtue does not seem to lie in the middle but beyond?

And how would it be possible to bestow on the great saints the halo of supreme virtue, which should stand exactly in the middle, without leaning to one extreme or the other?

Certainly, if the Church had had to canonize Christ, the Devil's Advocate would have had plenty of material for accusing Him of imprudence and fanaticism.

If all the children of the Church had practiced the diplomatic prudence that places virtue in the middle ground, she would have had no martyrs.

Wouldn't it be true to say that our mediocrity, our lack of the Holy Spirit, our laziness, and our middle-class mentality rather than our holy prudence have made us coin the axiom that virtue lies in the middle ground?

When I look at Christ, His Mother and the great martyrs and saints of history, I think that virtue lies rather in the extremes, that it is out head, in the vanguard, and to the left. The scandal of the cross embraces rather than renounces that love which is like a fire, always burning and in every direction.

Virtue is always non-conformist because it always wants something more, something better.

Virtue lies on the left, in opposition, because it does not admit that anything can be absolute, because it is always thinking that the possibility of something better lies beyond what we now have, however good that may be, because the riches of God are never exhausted.

Virtue does not rest on its oars but is dynamic; it is the salt that wards off corruption; it is the fire that nourishes all great hope.

Water that does not flow becomes stagnant, and hence virtue always pushes forward.

By its very nature, virtue is radical because it is not satisfied with particles of truth but seeks for truth itself.

We usually label as "extremists" those who go out ahead of the crowd, but the ancient prophets always lived beyond their own times, preparing for the future.

We cannot be real citizens of the present unless we are already contemporaries of the future. We are new every moment because God is continually born in us.

To say "That's enough!" is to sit down, surrender one's weapons and pretend to be God.

Searching continuously means to be on one's feet, feel alive and be hungry for God, always asking for more.

All the great deeds and movements of history have opened up fresh furrows and created something new while still retaining their revolutionary force. But when they sought the "center" and looked for compromise, they stopped being "salt" and "fire."

And this is true in every sphere—in politics, religion, culture, art and science.

When we speak about the middle-class mentality in movements or ideas, aren't we really talking about the desire to make virtue lie in the middle?

The founders of movements have always been more revolutionary and radical than their followers.

Prophets have always been more persecuted and misunderstood and have always met with more opposition than have bureaucrats.

The saints were not persecuted and ill-treated for being saints but for being extremists and revolutionaries.

I don't mean to say that every fanatic or every revolutionary is a saint, but that every real saint must be a revolutionary because he must live to the full his communion with Christ, the greatest Revolutionary of all time.

Christ did not command His apostles to make concordats or to look for compromises that would militate against the authenticity and radicalism of the Gospel. Instead, He told them: "They will persecute you. . . . They will deliver you up to councils and flog you in their synagogues. . . . If anyone will not receive you, shake off the dust from your feet as you leave that house or town."

I do not hereby wish to criticize those who, in the Church of today, suffer from the burden of an anti-Gospel tradition which cannot be shrugged off in an hour.

But I am criticizing each and every one of us because we are all responsible for the fact that not even the Pope can be as free as he would wish. When Pope John XXIII said: "I am a prisoner in a golden jail," I found his words more tragic than humorous.

Even he, the most evangelical Pope in the history of the Church, had to accept and sign concordats which he surely did not want. But he never ceased to scandalize some people with his personal fidelity to the Gospel.

Today we criticize the radicalism of Communist China in not allowing the least concession to "bourgeois imperialism." But perhaps tomorrow we shall admit that that radicalism was an alarm bell, a grain of salt that prevented certain fundamental values of the human community from being corrupted by what we in the consumer society are always trying to do.

The fact that revolutionary extremists may have to retrace their steps in order to regain their true path does not mean that they should take the road of the "center," but rather that they should start out again on their trail-breaking advance and their real revolutionary journey.

Every arrival point is a conquest, but it is also a new point of departure from which to penetrate deeply into the irreversible process of history, which is the very process of Christ.

We shall end our lives and still not have revolutionized the world enough. There will always be possibilities for advancing. There will always be things to discover. Men's fear will always be greater than their courage, and there will always be more people sitting around doing little or nothing of any consequence than are out hacking new paths through the jungle of the future.

CHRIST SAVES THOSE CONDEMNED BY THE LAW

I know that some of you do not share my faith, but that is precisely what urges me to speak frankly about my inmost convictions. For only thus can we set up a useful dialogue, such as I have always wanted in my conversations with friends who do not share my views and who say that they are far from my faith. Only in this way can I get to know, freely and frankly, their deepest reasons for their non-belief.

I believe that only if we communicate to each other the best that it is us, the deepest and most convincing reasons for our points of view and ways of life—only then shall we be able to speak to each other and, above all, to come together, discover each other, complete each other and examine each other's position, or at least to look into each other's eyes without fear and without contempt.

I am not ashamed to admit that my non-believing friends have helped me in a special way to revise my faith, purify my deepest beliefs and to discover new possibilities.

It was they who, for example, brought home to me with great clarity how grateful I should be for a faith that I would never have been able to acquire by my own powers alone. And they showed me the silly pride of my immature dogmatism and the ridiculousness of some of my angelistic pretensions. They taught me how to know Christ better because they obliged me to think deeply about the Christ whom we have not yet dared to preach—the Christ of the weak and the oppressed, of those who are nothing. Finally, my unbelieving friends have helped me to free myself from a type of theology formed by the stained hands of those who have used the Son of Man to justify and defend and even to bless the injustices and selfishness of the powerful ones of the earth who have subjected the weak to their whims, ambitions and self-serving demands in the very name of the faith.

I have the greatest respect for many of those who do not share my faith, for I have felt their sincerity, their courage in looking for the truth, their freedom from hypocrisy and their repugnance at the use of men as mere instruments. They have made me feel as weak as a child, and I have often thought that, without the mysterious and entirely unearned gift of my faith, I would not have very much of the human riches in which they abound.

I must say all this because I feel bound in justice to proclaim that I owe the truth in which I believe and which I love at least partly to the example of honesty which they have given me. Therefore, I have always considered as a kind of blasphemy the fact that many of those who go around proclaiming their faith in a God who became man so that man might become God, that these very people should be less just, less free, more grasping, more "common" and less human than those who are faithful to their own consciences and believe that no One greater than the earth has ever set foot on it. A Marxist friend of mine who was starting out as a journalist once said to me: "I'd like to know how a writer who is a Christian man feels free to write what he likes."

I cannot deny that my friend's question impressed me, for he was an honest man. That was the first time I felt the need to think about Christ as a "writer," so that I could prove I was free.

Then I remembered that our Lord had indeed done some writing but, so far as we know, only once, and then it was in the dust on the floor of the Temple in Jerusalem. Nobody knows or ever will know what He wrote or who erased those words that were the first letter written to men by God's own hand. But although no one knows these words that Christ wrote on the ground, we do know the result they had: they saved a woman from death by stoning at the hands of self-appointed, hypocritical judges; they taught later generations that permitting oneself the luxury of judging someone mercilessly is a much graver sin than committing adultery; that it is not sin which condemns a man definitively but rather the lack of faith in the rebirth of mankind, which presupposes a lack of faith in Him who has created and redeemed men.

In my opinion, the Bible incident that is richest in religious humanism is the one of the woman taken in adultery and dragged by the Scribes and Pharisees to the Temple, where Christ was teaching the revolutionary doctrine of the liberation of man: "The Son of man came to seek and to save the lost"; "Those who are well have no need of a physician, but those who are sick."

The Church herself has always been tempted to reduce the mercy of Christ and to take the part of those who thought it just and normal to stone the woman taken in adultery. For a long time, the Church was scandalized by this Gospel narrative to such an extent that originally it did not form part of the Gospel of St. John. It is lacking in the most ancient Greek manuscripts, the primitive Syriac versions and in the Coptic versions as well. On the other hand, however, it is found in some manuscripts of the ancient Latin version.

The passage was practically unknown to the Greek ecclesiastical writers until the eleventh century, but the Latins knew about it from the time of St. Ambrose in the fourth century. Nevertheless, the narrative comes from a very ancient tradition, and its historical authenticity is indisputable.

Accordingly, the Council of Trent admitted it definitively to the Canon of Holy Scripture.

A modern biblical scholar says that the passage was probably not accepted at first among the canonical Gospels because it seemed irreconcilable with the rigid discipline of the Church in regard to the sin of adultery.

But even today, in spite of the fact that the Church has no doubt about the authenticity of the passage, many Catholic theologians avoid it; it is not often used as a subject for sermons, and the full force of its argument has not yet been brought out.

The Scribes and Pharisees, those men of the law, crossed swords with Christ, the Friend of mankind. They whom He had held up as examples of hypocrisy and legal formalism followed Him around trying to catch Him out, whereas the ordinary people went to listen to Him and to bless the day He came among them. Accordingly, the Scribes and Pharisees tried to take advantage of the incident of the adulterous woman in order to trap our Lord. They were "scandalized" by His gentleness towards sinners and towards human weakness, and they intended to use this incident as an opportunity to propose a complicated case to Him.

The Law allowed an adulterous woman to be executed by stoning, but in this case Christ might perhaps go against the decree of Moses, and if He didn't, then the people would no longer regard Him as merciful. Christ's enemies thought, with good reason, that they had Him on the horns of a very difficult dilemma.

So they said to Him: "Teacher, this woman has been caught in the act of adultery. Now in the law Moses commanded us to stone such. What do you say about her?" (Jn 8:4-5).

All eyes were turned on Christ, as everyone waited for His answer. The Scribes and Pharisees were standing tensed and ready to leap on their prey, Christ was seated and the woman was in the middle, as it were between two fires.

Christ did not stand up and refused even to look at His enemies, with the instinctive repugnance of the Son of Man when confronted by those who were debasing the image of man, daring to condemn another human being made of the same clay as they.

"Jesus bent down and wrote with his finger on the ground," the Evangelist tells us.

Angered by Christ's scornful attitude, the Scribes and Pharisees obstinately insisted on an answer. Thye were eager to have Him compromise Himself, and perhaps they may have intended to stop Him from writing things that were beginning to cut them to the quick, while they still pretended not to understand what He was doing.

Finally, Christ stopped writing and, raising His eyes and glancing back over what He had written, He said: "Let him who is without sin among you be the first to throw a stone at her."

Then He bent down again and went on writing, perhaps about things that were more explicit, more personal, more telling. This time however, they did not dare to press their demand for an answer nor did they dare even to remain there: "They went away, one by one, beginning with the eldest." Soon there were only two people left, Christ and the woman, innocence and sin, the Creator and the creature, power and weakness, life and death, freedom and slavery. Christ was the freest of men. He would show by shedding His blood the great value He placed on each man; and He taught us that man's dignity has its roots in what he is and not what he has, and that the greatness of God consists in saving and not in condemning. Now He was confronted by this humbled, repentant woman, the living image of all the weak humans of history who had been condemned, not for being more sinful than their judges, but because they were less powerful and more defenseless. And what was His reaction? He who had barely deigned to glance at the woman's accusers, now stood up as a mark of respect for her repentant and humiliated frailty.

He had not done this for the Scribes and Pharisees, the great ones of Israel, the judges of the sinful woman. He had looked at them to shame them, whereas now He looked on her to redeem her and restore to her all her human and divine dignity.

"Has no one condemned you?"

"No one, Lord."

This is the first time we hear the woman speaking. When confronted by her judges, she had not dared to defend herself: she knew quite well that neither excuses nor the plain truth would be of any use as a defense before these men who were not looking for justice but for vengeance and for a chance to use her for their own evil purposes.

But she did speak to Christ. Perhaps, crouched on the ground as she was, she had been the first to read what He had written and saw in it her "absolution."

"Neither do I condemn you; go, and do not sin again"; that is, do not renounce your true liberty and dignity a second time.

Even Christ, who had the right to throw the first stone at her because He alone was truly innocent, did not undertake to condemn her.

The only time He wrote during His whole life, He did so to save a life, to defend a human being who had no one to protect her and to oppose those who had set themselves up as judges with their sentence of death already decided upon.

He wrote to lay bare the hypocrisy of those who had dared to judge by appearances and to condemn a human being, while He, the Lord of heaven and earth, said that even He had not come to judge: "Neither do I condemn you."

Christ here showed Himself as the truly free man who did not allow Himself to be entrapped by the intrigues of powerful men and as the true Son of Man for whom the law, which will always be necessary and which therefore He did not wish to destroy, is at the service of man and not man at the service of the law. The first time that Christ decided to write, He did so to save someone who had been condemned by the law.

He was, and is, Wisdom placed at the service of man's redemption.

He was, and is, Innocence putting itself at the service of human weakness, not to be contaminated by it, but to enlighten it with His light and strength.

Most likely the adulterous woman was present also when Christ exclaimed: "I am the light of the world; he who follows me will not walk in darkness, but will have the light of life" (Jn 8:12). His written words have been a light and have been capable of giving light to all those who are on the brink of death and desperation.

His words are a light which have warmed and embraced all those who recognize their own coldness, darkness, solitude, poverty, powerlessness and nakedness; while these same words of His have been darkness, harshness and an affront for all those who are capable of condemning a human being instead of saving him and who have rendered themselves unable to appreciate the beauty of the pearls which, in Christ's own severe words, should not be cast before swine.

Christ wrote on the ground because the ground itself cries out in defense of man, who is the kind of creation; and He did so in order to save man, not only spiritually, but also corporally.

In fact, Christ did not simply bless the adulterous woman, pardon her sins and then leave her to die under a hail of stones. He saved her life, and did it without having recourse to spectacular miracles but merely by the power of His words written in the dust, by His moral force as a prophet and with the splendor of His own innocence: "Which of you convinces me of sin?"

For that reason, from the moment I discover that Christ, on the first and only occasion when He wrote, did it to free a poor woman from death, to compel her judges to pardon her sin and to teach them that conscience is above the law and that man should not be crushed by any law that goes against his very nature, denying him all possibility of rebuilding his life—from that moment, I understood that the fact of my being a Christian not only did not lessen my freedom as a writer but gave it new dimensions.

From that moment, having Christ in my life has helped me to discover more clearly the demands of freedom that stirred my conscience, and to concern myself, both as a man and as a Christian, with the defense of man and with his being free from all slavery.

Whatever hindrance I may have found in my life as a writer, it did not come from the Christ of my faith but from certain social and religious structures which, instead of drawing inspiration from the Christ who frees, have used Him to block the most legitimate demands of freedom.

I have understood that it is truth that makes me free, and that Christ has sent me to cry out the truth "from the housetops."

I know that the love of God does not exist without love of my fellowmen, of any one of my brothers whatsoever, even the most nameless one in the street.

I know that Christ gave His own life for that nameless, insulted, humiliated, sin-ridden man.

I know that Christ was raised on the Cross simply because of those few words that he wrote during His life, because, although the Scribes and Pharisees slunk away ashamed on that occasion, they were not converted but were ever more eager to find another chance of killing Him.

I know that, as a Christian, I can reject as anti-Christian everything that can alienate a man.

I know that there are no limits confining me to any human dimension, either physical or spiritual.

I know that Christ Himself has taught me that no external law of my Church-structure can override with Him the imperious voice of conscience, which is the clear echo of the first word that the Creator wrote in my heart.

And because He has taught me by His own example, I also know that in a conflict between the law and the salvation of one man, I must choose the salvation of that man.

A certain magistrate, before joining a political party, asked: "In the case of conflict between the party and my conscience, which must I choose?" and he was told: "The Party!"

But he chose his conscience and did not join that party. I can joyfully affirm that, if I asked my Church this question, she would have to reply in the name of Christ Himself: "Your conscience!" Therefore, as a Christian, I can and must contribute to man's awareness of his freedom, that is, of his deepest being.

If I do not do so, not only am I not a real writer, but I am not a Christian writer, because it is precisely Christ who assures me that man can find his lost freedom. And regaining that lost freedom is a battle in which not only must honor and wealth be risked but even life itself, because, since Christ became man, I cannot feel free while even one man is a slave. My freedom begins where the freedom of others begins and not where their freedom ends.

THE TEMPTATION TO CHANGE OTHERS

Man can fulfil himself completely only if he is allowed to be "in the image of God."

And to be in the image of God, it is not necessary for him to know God as such.

Because every man finds within himself a force that urges him to be like the One who created him.

The words of St. Augustine: "You have made us for yourself, O Lord, and we shall not rest until we rest in You," are still very applicable in the field of psychology.

Actually, man continually feels himself drawn by something beyond him, by something that lives within him and yet is distinct from him.

Every man who is really alive feels the need for "more."

Basically, all men have a vocation from God, even those who deny and reject it.

A satisfied man is only half a man.

As St. John says: "He who does not love is dead," whereas love is dynamic, conquering, creative and forward-looking.

When a man says that he "wants to be himself," that he wants to "fulfil himself," he is really saying that he wants to be able to succeed in being everything toward which his interior tension, his deepest desire and his most legitimate hope are urging him.

But every profound desire and every true hope are born of the God who lives within us, who existed before us and who creates and sustains our very existence.

To be like the One who has created me is at once a need and a right.

But if every man has a right to be like God, then every man must respect this right in others.

Hence no one can try to make man, or permit him to be made, into the image and likeness of anyone else. No one can try to take the place of the Creator in this work, which is man's most sacred task.

Yet we have so few real images of the living and creating God, of the inexhaustible God, because we have committed the grave sin of trying to form men in our own image and likeness.

This is an abuse of authority that cries to heaven for vengeance.

And this sin has many levels. It begins in the very bosom of the family and later extends to all human authority and power.

We are touched when we see the child imitating its father or mother even in the way it holds its head; when we hear converts on the missions praying in our language; when the disciple becomes a perfect copy of the master; when the subject becomes the mechanical replica of the superior.

But since God is Infinite, there exist infinite possibilities for the image of God, possibilities which are both a proof and a product of His inexhaustibility.

Some years ago, I was particularly struck by two statements, the first being that of a famous Russian psychologist who affirmed that there are not and never will be two mothers who love their children equally, and the second statement, by a German theologian, to the effect that no two Christians have identical pictures of Christ in their hearts.

All of us are different despite the fact that the same current of life and love runs through us, and any attempt to smother this truth would be an insult to the Creator.

Every man has the right to be different so that he can be a unique image of the Creator, and he has the right to have this difference respected and untouched.

The Creator has given no man and no institution the mission or the authority to mold another man into his or its own image and likeness. Even Christ Himself did not have that mission. He never said: "Be like me!" but rather: "Be perfect as your heavenly Father is perfect." At most, He said: "Learn of me!" that is to say, learn to free yourselves of everything that prevents you from being yourselves, from being free, from searching to know the will of the Father, from being that unique image of the Creator, an image that cannot be repeated.

As proof of this it is enough to observe that although the apostles were formed by Christ Himself, each one of them kept his own personality and characteristics to a surprising degree until the last moment of his life. Christ did not mass-produce His apostles; He merely instructed them and then sent them forth to find their own way in the light of His grace.

At first glance, the idea of forming others in our own image and likeness seems simple and quite acceptable. But, in practice, even a little knowledge of history or of modern times is enough to show the terrible abuses and appalling crimes that have been committed by men and institutions in molding other men to their own image.

The man who is incapable of being free tries to make everyone else slaves.

The man who is afraid of love wants to shrivel up the hearts of all other men.

The man who does not know how to live without dominating others maintains that men have been created to obey and not to make new things and reach communal decisions in the name of Him who gave them the command to be "kings" of everything that exists.

The man who can envision a Church made up of people of only one color wants Christians to believe that Christ is that color and no other.

The man who cannot understand that an idea better than his own may exist makes himself incapable of a dialogue and a human relationship with his fellowmen for their mutual enrichment.

In fact, the first requirement for creating lines of communication with others is the conviction that no one is complete because we are all "images" of God but that no one is God, and that every human being possesses his own, unique riches which he can communicate to others.

Since, as the psalmist says, each man is almost a God, then each and every one of us possesses his own riches, whether they be hidden or manifest.

No man can substitute for another, and Peter will never be able to give me what Paul must.

Truly, each man needs to receive from other men and live in communion with them if he is to fulfil himself as he should.

Perhaps this is what we mean when we say that Christ is the only perfect, complete and definitive man who sums up in Himself the whole of humanity.

And only He is in vital communion with each and every man and with creation itself. Therefore, He contains within Himself the sum total of all the individual riches of men.

A really human and creative dialogue is impossible without this faith and this hope that each man who walks beside me brings me a new image of God, a different facet of love and a unique participation in the great mystery of humanity.

Obviously, in this context the statement made by the author of the *Imitation of Christ* does not hold true: "Every time I have gone among men, I have returned less a man." Instead, I think it is sound Christianity to say here: "Every time I communicate with another man, I am more like

Christ." Accordingly, we ought to be very cautious in our inborn desire to want to change everyone else instead of accepting them as they are. When I meet someone new, my first impulse should be to respect him and accept him as he is without falling into the temptation of thinking that I ought to change him because of the mere fact that he is not like me.

It is easy to think that anything that does not square with our own ideas is "negative," "undesirable" and hence to be corrected.

The sad realities of life teach us that in most cases what we wanted to change because it was different from our own way of thinking was really of greater value than, or at least was valuable in a different way from, what we possessed.

Therefore, accepting others as they are is not only demanded by the respect we must have for the consciences of other people, even when these consciences are erroneous, but is above all a duty that springs from our faith in the rich diversity of every man.

Ordinarily, what separates men from each other and prevents communication between them is ideology and sometimes even religion, understood as the institutionalization of faith, while, on the other hand, what unites them is the sincere will to enter into meaningful communication with each other.

Therefore dialogue must take place especially on the human level, on the level of existential communication.

Ideologies are what they are and they do not change. They may die, but they don't change. Yet the people who embody now or have in the past embodied an ideology can change. Love is the only thing that can make men equal and different at the same time, and love is deeper and more consistent than any ideology.

Therefore Christianity, not as a religion but as a faith whose driving force is love, can embrace in one community all men of every ideology and culture so long as they do not deny that love is the ultimate dimension of everything and everybody. Hence Christianity is not a creed but faith in an historical Person who died and rose again and who continues to be alive and present in history as the very power of love itself.

But if I am to enter into communication with my neighbor, it is not enough for me to accept by faith that he is different and that he possesses a richness distinct from mine. Instead, I must plunge into the dynamic current of love for him and for what he holds dear.

People are not self-contained units, living apart from and untouched by what they do, what they love and what surrounds them. Men are neither disembodied spirits nor mass-produced robots. Each man is himself plus his world, himself plus his tears, himself plus his hopes, himself plus his public and private life. Therefore, if I want to communicate with my neighbor, I must love him fully and show him the trueness of my love for him and for what he holds dear.

It would be futile, for example, to try to communicate with a mother if I did not also love her children; if, for instance, I excluded her son whom she loves as dearly as life itself.

I cannot love a friend and be indifferent to his friends.

It is not possible to enter into a real dialogue with an artist if I do not make it plain to him that I also love his pictures, statues, music, plays or films.

I cannot love the farmer if I do not love his land, cattle and sheep.

I cannot communicate with the man who thinks that I despise his religion, nor can I communicate with the unbeliever if I do not love the sincerity of his unbelief and in some way make it mine.

And I must do all this, not by way of strategy or out of diplomacy, which would be blasphemous, but really and sincerely.

Actually, if I truly love the person who is before me, I will feel attracted by his world and will love what he loves. When we love someone completely, we also love his world although we knew nothing about it until we met him, and we must make this a universal principle of action if our love for our neighbor and our desire to communicate with other men is to be sincere.

Communication is always an effort to eliminate obstacles so that we may penetrate as deeply as possible into the other person's world. But each man's world is terribly delicate, sacred, fearful and complex.

Man still carries with him much of the primitive fear of the jungle. He does not trust others easily and is suspicious by nature. Consequently, our approach to others must be very delicate lest we wound them, or impose ourselves, or humiliate or dominate them. Man is always a mixture of powerlessness and self-sufficiency. Almost instinctively, he rejects anything that is perfect, for fear that it may overpower or crush him, or that it may not help him solve his problems. Hence God's coming on earth as man, with all our limitations except sin, was a great act of wisdom.

In Christ, God made Himself understandable, acceptable, lovable, and a friend.

A God who wept, who had to flee from a tyrant, who felt the need to take refuge in the warmth of friends, who was so overcome by fear that He sweated blood and who felt abandoned at the supreme moment of death is a God who no longer terrifies weak, fragile man. Therefore, when we open our hearts to someone, sincerely and without pretence, we do not hinder but rather help communication with him.

When my neighbor knows that I, too, am limited, when he sees that I, too, am only a traveller on the road of life, that I do not have the solutions to many problems and that the answers that I do have are not overly dogmatic, he will easily open his heart to me in hope and friendship, and so there will be a greater possibility of building up between us a community of honest search. Then He will know that he, too, may be able to give me something, to enrich and enlighten me.

In addition to having the freedom of spirit to show my neighbor my weaknesses, I must also have the generosity of not concealing the good things I see in him and to help him discover the riches he possesses.

Basically, every man has little faith in himself despite all appearances to the contrary. Therefore we are all deeply grateful when someone really believes in us and shows us nice things about ourselves which we never knew we had.

These thoughts on Christian existential communication with our neighbor may cause some people to ask: "What do I need such communication for? Why must I enter into a dialogue with my fellowman?"

The younger generation is especially aware of the need for communication with the neighbor, and they show this awareness in the modes of expression they ordinarily use in their groups, clubs and friendships. Personally, I believe that this need for communication is not a passing phase but springs from man's very nature. Nowadays we are more conscious of this need, and we understand better than before that a man cannot be really human without other men.

A man who is physically or spiritually alone will always be an incomplete man.

Every sociologist, whether he is a believer or not, admits that man was created to fulfil himself through other men. But for the Christian, this need is more than a human one, for it is born of the very mystery of God's own life.

Man can be truly human only when he is an image of the Creator. But it is a dogma of faith that our God is not a "hermit." He is a "community" in Himself, for He is a

"Trinity." There exists in God a real community in which the Members keep Their own Personalities in the highest degree. They are three "distinct" Persons, but They are so closely united with each other that They form a Unity, so that we can only speak about *one* God and not about three, for this is a perfect, total union created by love.

Now, it is this God, who is not a hermit but a community, who created man "in his own image and likeness," that is to say, He created him in such a way that he must be in a community if he is to be truly human. But, unlike God, man cannot accomplish this by himself but must do so with the help of his neighbors.

If a man denies this dimension of his humanity, he refuses to be a man. Therefore communication between men on all levels is a need and not just a fashion; it is a necessity and not merely a duty; it is a right which he acquires when he is created.

"YOU ARE GODS"

Aided by the Holy Spirit in its continual search, the people of God is constantly throwing new light on one or other of the truths which God has revealed to man.

This, however, does not mean that the people of God denies or belittles other truths which, at other times, were in the forefront of the Church's consciousness. Instead, it shows that man always needs to go on searching in every field, not excluding the field of faith; it means that he always feels the goad of the infinite and that, far from being a curator of a museum of fossilized facts, he is called to open up new paths and penetrate into hitherto untouched territory. And this vocation of man's to be an explorer is continually stimulated by the Spirit of God, who breathes in man when He wills and as He wills, although the degree to which He does this will always be measured by man's generosity in following his vocation as an explorer.

And we must be very conscious of this fact whenever the people of God feels urged to deepen its knowledge of certain truths which, while they never were denied, still have never been investigated in all their depth and terrible grandeur.

For example, the theological consequence of the dogma of the Incarnation is one of the truths which are being revealed with increasing clarity and depth, frightening some people and making others very enthusiastic.

Christ is the God who became man in order that man could discover and live the tremendous reality of being a "god."

The Word of God became man so really in Christ that more than a few people find it difficult without the help of the Faith and from Scripture alone, to prove that He was really God and not merely a special envoy sent by Him to mankind. But, at the same time, man is discovering that he is so identified with Christ, so really Christ, so truly the son of God by reason of the Incarnation and the Resurrection, that he is terrified to acknowledge that this is so. And after twenty centuries, we are still afraid to assert and cry aloud triumphantly that we are Christ, that we are gods.

We still carry upon our shoulders the burden of the fear which our first parents felt when, having tried to usurp the majesty of God by eating the forbidden fruit, they not only failed to do so but were stripped of even their higher human privileges as a punishment.

But, as an old blind hermit said to me some years ago, we have forgotten "that the very thing that man wanted to arrogate to himself against God's will has been offered to him freely by God as a supreme gift of love. In Christ, man is turned into God, into a son of God: he is Christ." And he added: "Therefore, I do not consider that I am blind because when a person sees this great truth clearly, he is already living in God's light and is able to taste real happiness."

When we say that man is Christ, and hence that he is God, we do not mean that a person who discovers that he is God in Christ is then unable to rebel against God the Father. On the contrary, it is at that precise moment of supreme greatness that man can consciously reject his Creator: I can really rebel against someone only when I am on the same plane as that someone; I can prefer myself to God—which is the essence of Hell—only when I feel that I really am a son of God, "another Christ."

Christ, who was the Word of God, the Son of God, also

had to submit Himself to the will of His Father, and He sweated blood with the effort of making His will conform with that of His Father. Even though Christ was truly God and equal to His Father in all things, as man He was dependent on His Father; and in us, who are God in Christ, there exists the dependence of creation and redemption.

But we do not thereby cease to be gods, to be Christ Himself.

Parents who beget a son of their own flesh and blood make him as much a "man" as they themselves are by a free act of love. In the son there always exists a dependence of love and gratitude upon those who have given him the ability to be a human as they are. But this dependence does not prevent him from being as truly "man" as his parents are.

We "are born of God"; God really begets us and makes us gods. If man were not really God, God would not have been able to become man. It is impossible to imagine God becoming incarnate in a dog or a flower. A dialogue of love can be started, without hypocrisy and without going against nature, only between beings of the same species. If man were not God, God could not enter into a dialogue with him, and He could not call man "friend" and "son." God will never enter into a dialogue with a whale unless He first makes it a god, a member of His own race.

Christ Himself told His followers: "You shall do greater things than those I have done." Is it possible for a man to do greater things than those which Christ did unless Christ is with him and is like him?

Christ also said that the Holy Spirit "will show you all things." But can anyone reveal all his most intimate secrets to someone who is not on his own level?

God has loved us with all His tremendous capacity for love. Therefore, the mere fact of entering into a dialogue of love with God would have made us gods. But Christ

Himself reminds us that, from the very beginning, God created man a "god." This is one of the most significant passages in the Gospel of St. John, one which hitherto we have kept too much in the background.

In the tenth chapter of St. John's Gospel, we read how scandalized the Jews were when Christ said that He and the Father were "one" (Jn 10:30), thus revealing Himself as God. When the Jews accused Him of blasphemy, Christ defended Himself by asking ironically: "Is it not written in your law, 'I said you are gods'?" (Jn 10:34; Ps 81:6). And He went on to say: "Scripture cannot be broken" (Jn 10:35).

This was as if to say: "You are scandalized because I say that I am the Son of God, identical with the Father: yet it is written in the Scriptures that God Himself has stated that all of you are gods." And His declaration, "Scripture cannot be broken," is very graphic, as if He were saying: "Although you may be scandalized, and although you may never have understood or believed it, God really has called you men 'gods'."

I do not know if we have thought enough about the fact that Christ Himself, with all His authority, interpreted the most tremendous statement of the whole Bible: the fact that God has made man a real "god."

Even the words of Genesis, "God created man in his own image and likeness," should be interpreted in the light of this psalm, in which the Holy Spirit places in God's mouth an even more radical affirmation: "You are gods." And Christ confirmed this with all His authority when He accused the Jews of blindness because they were scandalized at Him for claiming to be the firstborn Son of the Father, when in reality all men are true sons of God.

However, although this truth could have frightened men before the coming of Christ, after the Incarnation Christianity should have been more aware of this "identification" with Christ. Nevertheless, we Christians have often been most afraid of facing up to this truth, which could have freed the world from its chains and revealed to it its terrible but joyful grandeur and dignity. Instead, we have given the completely contrary impression, that of wanting to convince the world, through our Faith, of man's littleness, uselessness and continued lack of maturity; of the great distance between him and God; and of his status as a slave standing before his Creator.

And it is painful to admit that at times quite a few people outside Christianity, or who have no faith at all, have been the very ones who were the first to glimpse intuitively —whether for good or evil—that man can do things which, until recently, we thought were exclusive to God's direct personal action.

Perhaps without believing or even knowing about Christ's words, "You shall do greater things than those I have done," they have really believed in man's ability to continue the work of creation, perfecting it, dominating matter and transforming it in numberless ways, entering into the deepest mysteries of man himself, and not stopping with any conquest of science, no matter how spectacular or incredible it might be.

Today we know that man possesses the capability and probably even the means of destroying the very work of the Creator, while all the animals on earth together could not change by one hairsbreadth the rhythm of nature or of the cosmos.

Today man can begin to destroy creation; he can disintegrate matter; he can change man's own nature by manipulating the very core of life itself.

That's terrible, you'll say. But it is also magnificent!

Today there are no longer any limits for science, and even the mystery of death does not seem to be eternally reserved to God's direct action, for it seems possible that man may succeed one day in conquering biological death by means of science.

The unbeliever does not find it difficult to think that man possesses, at least in potency, the very power of God.

But the believer can go only as far as accepting the fact that God has really created man a "god," with all the consequences, the most terrible of which is the power to rise up against Him and His work and refuse to enter into a dialogue of love through Christ, with whom every man is identified.

But along with the natural fear of the man who discovers that he is a "god," the Christian must also experience the ecstatic joy of acknowledging that he is "Christ," of knowing that he is seated at God's own table, of discovering that he is infinite, that he can speak of Him as a friend and love Him truly with the same love with which He loves Himself and us.

WHY WE ARE AFRAID

We are still afraid of freedom, and therefore powerful interests are more easily able to enslave us. They will never come right out and say that they are trying to curtail our freedom but rather will pretend to protect it. If power structures are to retain their strength, they must foster in us those twinges of nostalgia for slavery that we still feel.

We have always loved our freedom as one of the greatest of boons, but at the same time we have carried on our shoulders for centuries the burden of fear. We love freedom, but we love order, peace and quiet still more.

When Moses was leading the sons of Israel from the slavery of Egypt to the freedom of the Promised Land, he discovered that the slaves did not always accept their liberators with open arms. They preferred the devil they knew to the "liberating angel" they didn't know, and the plagues of Egypt to the pangs of emancipation.

Similarly, when Christ cast out the devils from two possessed men and sent them into the herd of Gadarene swine, St. Matthew tells us that "all the city came out to meet Jesus; and when they saw him, they begged him to leave their neighborhood" (Mt 8:34). In a recent film of this incident, Christ is depicted as replying to this request of the Gadarenes: "What you want is to go on being slaves because you are afraid of freedom."

And it is a fact that, although we want to be free, we frequently allow ourselves to be very easily enslaved, both in civil as well as in religious matters.

Today every country that is even halfway developed wants to be democratic, and all the more so if it has had to bear the burden of oppression. Nevertheless, these nations have scarcely begun to pay the inevitable price of real freedom when they start to feel the stirrings of a nostalgic longing for the clear-cut "discipline," "order" and "efficiency" of the old dictators.

Those who love power know very well how to use this longing and this inborn weakness of man, which has been fed on his fears down through the ages. And they can operate so skillfully and so thoroughly that, even when a nation wakes up and wants to take over the full responsibility for its own freedom, it often finds it physically impossible to do so. This is the case today with the nations of Eastern Europe, and tomorrow it may be the lot of some of the Western European countries, too.

Yet we shall never reach our personal and collective maturity without being truly free. We cannot be persons without the real exercise of our freedom. We can be like God only when we are allowed to be free, because God is free and He created us in His own image, confiding to us all the responsibility of our freedom.

When God created us, He forbade us only one thing. He forbade us to renounce being ourselves, to renounce our own responsibility.

According to the biblical narrative, when the first man and woman disobeyed their Creator, they actually renounced being free and being themselves. They wanted to be like God. Rather than accept the commitment and personal responsibility of ruling the earth, they wanted to have their eyes opened and "be like God, knowing good and evil" (Gen 3:5). But they wanted all this to happen as if by magic, without any effort on their part, without any searching, without any self-compromise and completely passively.

But when we turn our back on being men, even in an effort to be God, we betray ourselves. Therefore, when God permits us to rise toward Him, He does not do it by obliging us to cease being men, but rather by becoming God through being perfect men in Christ.

God forbids us to have or to do only that which prevents us from being free. But when we want to imitate Him by planting forbidden trees in our earthly paradise, we abuse our power and fall into Adam's sin because, unlike the Creator, we do it to prevent other men from being themselves, to take away their freedom, to spare them the job of thinking and to save them from taking on the risk of responsibility.

We would even take away man's ability to sin, if we could.

But God never took this possibility from men, because if men cannot sin against God, they cannot love Him either.

Sin does not reside in the intellect, but in the will.

One can sin only against love.

But if we are to love, we must be free.

Freedom and love always go hand-in-hand.

And if we are to love deeply, we must be free and must be able to be ourselves at every moment.

Nobody can enslave a man who has discovered love, for love is stronger than force.

You can kill a man who loves, but you cannot make him submit.

Isn't this the reason why power fears love so much?

In fact, I have asked myself more than once why the totalitarian regimes, the inquisitorial power structures, both civil and religious, have always been the ones who most feared love. Totalitarian regimes, whether fascist, communist or imperialist, have always favored a so-called "rigorist" morality which represses even the most innocent manifestations of love.

To the extent that the Church has become a power structure, it has begun to reinforce the fences around every budding love and has been preoccupied about the breaking of only one commandment, which was not precisely the "new commandment" of Christ.

Hence she has been more interested in defending faith rather than hope, morality rather than love, obedience rather than freedom, and diplomacy rather than truth.

It is difficult to domineer over men who know the truth, because "the truth shall make you free."

And it is difficult to maintain a structure based on power when people have discovered that love is the root of everything and is its own final dimension, the ultimate reality before which not only the law but even conscience itself must kneel.

Love is the only thing that can give back to man his original freedom; it is the only thing that can finally erase in him the last vestiges of his ancestral fears, the only thing that can eliminate his remaining taboos and reveal him to himself.

Love does away with power because it does not seek to domineer but to offer itself in service.

A mother may suffer greatly when her daughter falls in love because she knows instinctively that love will make her daughter free and will place the girl outside her power. Her daughter will no longer be "hers."

Similarly, the Church suffers when her children find out that Christianity is the faith which reveals that love is the ultimate dimension of life and the only thing that saves; that there are no laws against love, because the Christian God is the God who has revealed that He is love itself, the God who will judge only according to the code of love, and the God who has revealed that men can organize themselves, live together and fulfil themselves without needing power and simply by being faithful to love.

The Church's power structure suffers when men discover this truth because she feels that her fortifications are being undermined and that she must resign herself to being a Church which is "one" but not "uniform." She must be "one" because love makes one sole being out of all those who love one another, but she is not "uniform" because love is always creative and always takes on the characteristics of each human being.

Since Christianity is a religion of love, the Church is a community of those who love and who have believed that the love revealed in Christ is the last dimension of all.

And since it is true that no two mothers love equally, and no two loves are exactly alike, then Christians, who are the prophets and revealers of love, can all be different from each other without ceasing to be a community of believers in love.

He who loves belongs to the Christian community.

He who rejects love does not belong to the Church of Christ.

The Eucharist that is celebrated by one small group of members of the Christian community in one house need not take the same outward form as that celebrated by another small group in the house next door. It is sufficient that both Eucharists be born of the same need to relive the same sacrifice of Christ's love by which He gave Himself for all men. In the Mass, it is the sacrifice of Christ that counts and not the language or ritual that enshrines it.

It is love that must give expression to the action. It is love that creates gestures and words to manifest itself, and not gestures and words that create love. A kiss or embrace does not create love and, of itself, it an empty sign. But if I genuinely love someone, this very love will inspire me to make the appropriate gesture to show that person my love.

If there is one thing clear in Christian dogma, it is that the law, by itself, does not justify or save men. Instead, it may even destroy them because "the letter kills" while the spirit, that is to say, love, "gives life."

Even a law that is made to protect the rights of the weak and the freedom of those who were enslaved is, of itself, ineffective without love. As Martin Luther King said, the law can enforce "toleration" between blacks and whites, but it cannot enforce "the brotherhood of man."

However, power and laws make it easier to govern and to maintain an established, static order which creates no problems. Power structures prevent man from discovering the heady taste of freedom and his own marvellous possibilities for love.

If we substitute love in place of the law, as Christ did, we make men free and eliminate power. Then even another Judas cannot be excommunicated, because the consciences of others must be respected; and the greatest among us will have to wash the feet of the least, because love makes us all equal. And then the new Judas will be able to betray you; and the least and last of all, like St. Paul among the apostles, will be able to say to the greatest, such as was St. Peter, that he is wrong.

Then there will be a greater possibility of martyrdom, and authority will become a burden and not a privilege.

Then the doors will be open to greater scandals, but also to heroic love.

But only then will men be free; only then will they freely accept the only restraints that have any value, those which protect against the corruption of love and freedom.

Washing my brother's feet, listening to him, admitting that he may be right and I wrong, obeying him in planning the liberation of all men, can be an act of slavery, a curtailing of my freedom, but it is a slavery that becomes a joy because it keeps love fresh and makes it possible.

The girl who gets into her finance's car on a Sunday afternoon and asks: "Where are we going today?" is really giving up her freedom and personal initiative, and becomes a slave, but her renunciation springs from love, from her need to give herself. It is confidence in the moral strength of one in whose love she believes and trusts. Today he is in the driver's seat, but tomorrow she will do the driving; tomorrow he will obey her, because to obey or be obeyed is, in this case, the same thing, because both have the same root in the deep love that unites them.

The Church must not get up in arms or fulminate wrathfully against those who may abuse this new dimension of authority based on the love of free men; or against those who will use her for their own selfish aims; or against the possible Judases who will take advantage of her lack of power to betray her and to give her into the hands of her enemies; or against those who will cackle with glee when they see her renouncing all power structures.

At the most, she can weep as Christ did; she can ask sorrowfully: "Are you betraying me with a kiss?"; she can exclaim, as Christ did to Peter: "Get behind me, Satan!" But she must respect each man's conscience and allow the wheat and the weeds to grow side by side. And she must have sufficient humility to realize that she is not Christ; that God is greater than she; that He always walks ahead of her; and that it will not always be easy for her to distinguish clearly between the wheat and the weeds, because this would demand that the eyes of her members and representatives should be as clear as those of the Master. But we know very well that the dust from all the roads of the world is constantly blowing into the eyes of the pilgrim Church on earth. Yet she will never be blinded, because Christ, whose eyes see into men's hearts, is also among the pilgrims, and it was He who asked that the wheat and the weeds be allowed to grow together because the final separation of the one from the other belongs to Him alone.

I have always been touched by the fact that Christ denied the Church the power to declare with authority that any one concrete person is an enemy of God, and much less that such a person has been irrevocably damned.

Only when the world and its structures have lost their fear of loving will men begin to be free.

Freedom is troublesome, but it is divine, just as love is the enemy of power but is liberating.

Christ's great commandment was not "Dominate one another!" but "Love one another!"

True Christians should repeat every morning the words of Thomas Jefferson: "I have sworn before the altar of God eternal enmity to every form of tyranny over the minds and hearts of men."

CHRIST HAS NO LOVE FOR PAIN

The statement, "God cannot exist because, if He did, He would be evil," is one of the most serious objections raised by atheists when confronted with the reality of pain.

Can there be a God while children and innocent people go on dying and while the most atrocious sufferings are the daily lot of so many human beings?

How is it possible for a God to exist who allows good men to suffer and evil ones to prosper and enjoy life to the full?

A God who is untouched by the sufferings of His children, and especially of those who are the weakest and most innocent, is a God that many people find impossible to accept.

Every religion that accepts the existence of a personal God has always tried mightily to answer this objection, which is certainly an empty one.

Christianity, too, has proposed answers which, however, haven't always satisfied the most demanding and critical enquirers.

Perhaps it would be more honest to say that, apart from the teaching of the Faith, we do not have any fully satisfactory answer. We believe in our God despite the pain in the world and its apparently unjust distribution.

However, I would like to speak about the danger of trying to "sanctify" pain or to "love" suffering, as a too simplistic answer to this tremendous problem.

In short, since we haven't been able to find an adequate

answer to the question "Why does God allow pain?" it
has often seemed logical to hold that pain is good and necessary for man.

And this temptation has been so real that we have even
taken the assumption a step further and said: "We ought
to seek out and even love pain." Then we have justified our
conclusion by citing the example of Christ, who suffered an
appallingly painful Passion and death. Thus was born "vic-
timistic" spirituality, which forces the text of St. Paul:
". . . in my flesh I complete what is lacking in Christ's afflic-
tions . . ." (1 Col 1:24).

In this way, pain, even physical pain, is raised to the
category of a "Christian good," and it is sometimes regarded
as the only good, the only thing that has any value in God's
eyes.

Pain is, therefore, seen as being good in itself or at least
in its effects, because it pleases God or helps us to be better
Christians.

Frequently the first act of religion we teach our children
is "to offer it up as a sacrifice for the Child Jesus."

And often we even surround prayer, our personal dialogue with God, with sacrifice so that it may be more pleasing to Him.

It is true that the Church has never taught that pain is
good in itself, but in practice this idea has been present in
our spirituality, our morality and even in our theology. For
example, the Eucharistic mystery has often been reduced to
the one category of sacrifice. Basically, what we have been
doing is reviving the theology of the pagan gods who are
pacified only by the blood of their victims; or, at most, we
have not gone beyond the first religion of Moses.

The God who said "I desire mercy and not sacrifice"
(Mt 9:13) has, in practice, been relegated to oblivion.

Our God is still the God who was placated by justice and
not by mercy; the God who created us to suffer and not to

enjoy things; the God who is always calling us to dwell in a valley of tears and not to live in a paradise.

But this is not Christian; it is not theologically correct; it is not even human.

And we must have the courage to say so, although we may thereby be left without any answer to the problem of pain.

We must have the courage to say that pain is not Christian; that God never loved pain; that we men have ourselves brought tears into the world, because in God there exists only happiness; and that He has not yet blessed the tears that we have sown throughout this earth of ours, which should be a paradise.

When Christ made His incredible act of love for men by becoming a man among men and for their sake, He had to accept all our human limitations.

Therefore, in taking our flesh, He also took on our burden of pain.

But Christ *bore* pain and never "loved" it.

He would have preferred not to have had to suffer.

Indeed, He found pain so repugnant that, when His Passion drew near, He sweated blood and begged His Father to spare Him the horror of death on the cross: "If it is possible, let this chalice pass from me." He did not say: "I bless you, Father, because you are giving me this opportunity to suffer and so show you my love," but rather: "Please, please, don't make me suffer so much!" And the Father did send angels to Him to console Him.

On the cross itself, moments before His death and overwhelmed by the most appalling sea of pain, of utter loneliness and abandonment by His Father, Christ did not say: "Thank you, Father, because you are making me taste the worst possible human pain!" Instead, He complained piteously about the awful anguish He was undergoing: "My God! My God! Why have you abandoned me?", as if to say: "I do not understand why you are making me suffer like this!"

One has only to read the Gospel to see that Christ found it hard to bear pain and welcomed it in others even less than in Himself. He was never a friend of sickness, and therefore all His miracles were worked to cure, to restore life, to give hope, to assuage hunger.

Not once did He say, when confronted by a specific case of suffering: "Be happy about your illness! Endure your hunger! Bear the pain of your son's death!"

He allowed His disciples to pluck ears of wheat on the Sabbath, that is to say, to break the Law, so that they would not go hungry. He never said to them: "Offer it up!"

The disciples of John the Baptist were scandalized because Christ's disciples did not fast, but He told them that His followers would have time to fast when He was gone, that is, when they would have no other recourse.

Christ did not come to raise pain to the status of a good; He did not come to bless or sanctify pain, but rather to teach us that pain must not drive us to desperation, because there are immensely more important values which not even pain can eliminate. Therefore He used to tell His disciples not to fear even those who could take away their lives.

Christ came to save man, to free him from every bond that could give him pain, because man's goal is happiness. He came to teach us the true dimension of happiness and to open its gates to us.

Christ came to reveal to us that if we want to buy the treasure of learning how to love—which is the same as entering His kingdom—we must be ready to sell all that we have, even our very lives.

He came to teach us that we can be truly men, and hence happy, only when we know how to open ourselves up to the last dimension, which is living for others, since we can be happy only with others and through them.

And in this respect it is worthwhile undergoing pain in order to enter into this vital current which will unerringly bear us along towards the only true happiness.

Christ Himself suffered in the crucible of pain so as not to renounce the dynamic of love. He certainly did not do so in order to teach us to suffer but to show us how to love.

Christ did not say to us: "Suffer as I have suffered!" but: "Love one another as I have loved you!" And love is the very source of joy.

Hence the Christian not only can but must work to try and conquer pain on earth, and he must not accept any pain other than that which necessarily follows from his need for love and his commitment to promoting the happiness of others. Therefore every truly human conquest is in reality another door opened to a world that has less pain in it and that is more like the final kingdom, where weeping will be no more.

The Christian's mission is to show men that love exists, that it is possible, that it has a name and that it is every man's only possibility for happiness.

Pain does not belong in our final home. When love will have blossomed in all its beauty and perfection, it will not be accompanied by pain, even as a sign of its authenticity.

Hence the man who is already rising from the death with Christ and who, with Him, has finally conquered death, has the right to conquer all physical and moral suffering, too. If this were not so, it would be immoral for the Christian to use medicine, to engage in works of mercy and even to pray for relief.

The Christian accepts pain without rebelling against His Father, but without loving it, and he is aware that he is travelling towards a happy state for which he is already preparing and in which all pain will be overcome.

Every moment of pain is one moment more of pilgrimage in time; every moment of joy is an anticipation of the promised land. Therefore it is lawful, it is even our duty to live in such a way that our normal attitude is one of happiness and self-giving love. We do not make pain our own nor do we consider it a value in itself, much less a permanent state.

When I feel pain, I bear it, but I go on looking for happiness: I do not stop to contemplate it, much less embrace it, for it is something that I do not consider mine.

Hence even in the midst of a very real pain, whether physical or moral, I can say that I am not suffering since I do not make pain one of my life's activities. I go on loving and striving so that other men may discover their dimension of happiness, so that they may be happier than I am right now, and so that they may be capable of loving. And perhaps my pain, which I do not love but only bear with, will spur me to greater efforts to rid others of pain.

Pain will probably always exist in this passing world because only with difficulty will men learn to love deeply, and because only love will eliminate pain.

We are the ones who daily sow pain throughout the world.

God sends us only the seeds of happiness.

Every time I have met someone who really loves, with the profound dimension of Christ, I have found it very hard to get him to say that he is suffering, because what I looked on as suffering was not so for him. Even when the suffering was very real, it was so unimportant in comparison to his love that he could truly say that he was not suffering at all.

There are people who live only to love and to reveal love to others, and they accept the consequent physical or moral pain as something natural which is submerged and lost in the current of their positive vitality.

One such person said to me: "Asking me if I am suffering is like asking a mother if she is suffering because she gave her hungry child her last crust of bread." Even when such a mother feels the pangs of hunger, she cannot say that she is suffering: she loves her child, and that is enough. But she would really suffer if she were compelled to eat the bread and leave her child hungry.

Obviously, only someone who loves can understand this.

I do not see how any pain that is not born of a need to give to others can have meaning in a healthy Christianity, based on the Gospel.

I canot understand why God would want and require man to look for and love pain because Christ accepted His Passion and death rather than betray His vocation as the Savior and Liberator of men. Quite the contrary: He suffered so that we might be happy and find once more the road to eternal happiness.

Christ did not choose death, and death on the cross at that, to show the world His love. He was simply killed by men. What touches me about Christ is His giving Himself for others without counting the cost. If He had died to defend an idea, He would have been a hero, but nothing more. Seeing Him on the cross is, for me, a guarantee of the authenticity of His love, but it is not absolutely necessary to convince me of His love.

His Mother did not die on a cross but in the happiness of her bodily Assumption into heaven, yet this does not make me less assured of her love for men. Who would dare to say that Mary loved her Son more at the foot of the cross than on that blessed night in the stable at Bethlehem?

He who loves, loves always, in happiness or in pain and sorrow. What counts is love. When love is real and deep, it does not stop at, or end in, sacrifice, because it is "stronger than death"; but love is a substantial value in itself and does not need pain to exist.

At the end of time, our food and our life will be love. yet every vestige of pain will have been wiped away.

Therefore, in reality, it is not pain that brings us close to

God, as is usually said, but love.

Pain has driven many people to suicide, while happiness has revealed God to others.

Similarly, it is not poverty that brings us near God but generosity and freedom from all slavery to things. Penury and want have driven many people to become atheists. It is not hunger that pleases God but the love that leaves itself without food for the sake of others. The mistaken idea that every form of happiness is selfish has made us think that only he who feels hunger is capable of understanding the hunger of others. Actually, the contrary is true: he who relishes his crust of bread as a necessary and pleasant boon, is precisely the one who should be most unwilling to tolerate the hunger of the poor.

Christ told us that we should love others as we love ourselves. Consequently, we must begin by loving ourselves and by loving everything that we have. If it were otherwise, Christ, who possessed the most love, who was the happiest and healthiest and most perfect of men, would have been the least capable of understanding the emptiness, loneliness, selfishness, sickness and brutality of other men. But it was precisely because He held the fire in His own hands that He wished the whole world to be ablaze, too.

It is true that, very often, those who are the poorest, weakest and most downtrodden are the most generous, the most self-sacrificing, the most understanding and human. But these are also the ones who are richest in love.

The poor man is more generous, not because he is poor, but because he loves more. If someone has a big bank account, it does not by any means always follow that he has a big heart, too, although we are often tempted to think so. Nor do wealth and intelligence necessarily go together; indeed, the contrary is normally the case.

Therefore, very often we Christians, by dint of sanctifying pain and even desiring it as good in itself, have been tempted to bestow it upon, and foster it in, others.

· And that is monstrous, and it has often made us hateful
and unworthy sons of the God of mercy, the God of happiness. It has also conveniently saved us the trouble of wip-
ing away many tears and of crying out against many injustices that hinder man from finding the way to happiness
and that sow suffering throughout the world.

More than once we have been struck dumb when confronted with the suffering of innocent children and good
men, and have consoled ourselves by saying that it makes
their salvation more certain and renders them more pleasing
to God.

But if I cannot force anyone to love, since love is the supreme act of man's freedom, much less can I compel anyone to suffer, and even less to suffer in the name of God, who
bore pain so that we might be happy.

I must help man to find the true path to happiness, which
is not the road of pain but of generosity. I must help them
to discover that one is happy only in loving, that only by
living for others can one take the sting out of pain, and that
every selfish attempt to spare oneself effort or suffering at
the expense of commitment to and communion with others
is to fall into the deepest and most insuperable pain.

Sometimes great pain has opened a person's eyes and set
his feet on the road of generosity, but in this case pain has
served only to show him the absurdity of his life and the
emptiness of his existence, despite all the appearances of
happiness.

On the other hand, the happiness of finding a sincere
love or a deep and generous friendship has converted others
and shown them how to break out of their selfish shell.

In the end, it is always the revelation and discovery of
real love that makes a man capable of consciously finding
himself, which is the beginning of freedom and the prelude
to true happiness. To deny that our destiny, even here be-

low, is happiness, would be to deny Christianity, and this holds good also for the view that we reach happiness alone and not in communion with others.

Canonizing pain is not accepting Christ but crucifying Him again.

THE FAMILY IN CRISIS

People are beginning to say that the traditional institution of the family, which is the primary, fundamental cell of the community, is in a state of crisis.

But, on the other hand, perhaps never before as today has there been in the Church more appreciation for the dignity and greatness of the marriage union. As a matter of fact, the renewal begun by the Second Vatican Council has removed almost all traces of Manichaeism and the taboos about sexuality and human love.

Why, then, are people beginning to think that the institution of the family may need a profound and even radical change precisely at the moment the Sacrament of Matrimony is more appreciated than ever before?

Are we sure that the accusations which are being levelled against the family as an institution come only from the liberal camp and the promoters of free love?

Or may there not exist in Christian circles, too, the conviction that something is changing or ought to change in the classical, traditional form of the primary Christian community?

I think that it is not easy to separate the two points of view and that the present institution of the family is really being brought up for questioning by both sides.

When we consider the human condition of men and women, their difficulty in reaching real maturity in love, their social and psychological circumstances and the large

proportion of selfishness that is always found in human attitudes; and when we consider further that the family, because of its greatness, both natural and Christian, always
presupposes a capacity for sacrifice since it is the total,
free and definitive gift of self to another—we can see that,
inevitably, the family as such will always have enemies of
every stripe.

A theologian has wisely remarked that God will always
be uncomfortable for those who are unable to regard love
as a giving of oneself to another. Therefore, it follows that
everything that participates directly in God's generous,
disinterested love will also be uncomfortable, especially the
union in marriage of a man and woman, which is the reflection of God's own love, that has given everything and
demanded nothing.

It would be naive to think about the family without taking into account the sacrifices of personal freedom that it
entails. A vision of the family as a romantic dream and a
perpetual honeymoon is possible only in the childish world
of young lovers or the unreal one of some unmarried dream-
ers.

Fathers and mothers of families all over the world know
very well that, while the family is founded upon human and
natural self-fulfillment and has supernatural possibilities that
are infinite, it also requires more than a little self-sacrifice,
self-surrender, self-renunciation and sometimes even dra-
matic conflicts.

The Two Objections

Among those who bring up objections against the institution
of the family today, there are two clearly marked schools
of thought. There are those who think that the institution
as such has become outmoded, and who, therefore, deny
its basic value and relevance; and there are others who believe that, although it is still the basic institution of the hu-

man community, it must nevertheless undergo a profound transformation.

The first school of thought denies in practice the possibility of a total and definitive encounter between a man and a woman. They deny that a man can fulfil himself if he is bound up in a lifelong partnership with the one woman, or a woman with only the one man. They also deny that a man is capable of making a choice in love that will be binding for the rest of his life. And finally they deny in principle that human love in itself tends toward fecundity.

Logically, this position cannot possibly be reconciled with Christianity, which has always seen in the union of a man and a woman the possibility of a mature, definitive encounter, to the point of sanctifying it as a Sacrament that is the symbol of Christ's love for and union with His Church.

Christianity has always believed that man and woman not only have the possibility of blending together and of collaborating with each other in building up this world, but also that of raising their human love to the level of the divine, grafting it on to God's own substantial love.

That is why Christianity has given so much importance to the words of Christ: "What God has joined together, let no man put asunder" (Mt 19:6). If God can unite a man and a woman, it is a sign that He believes it possible for them to blend together and create a true, human, definitive community out of only one couple.

But, while we accept the human and Christian reality of the family as a community that is perfect in itself, perhaps we should listen respectfully to those who are honestly convinced by the harsh experience of life that the Christian institution of the family needs to undergo a profound change.

It is not a question of discussing the institution as such, but only the way in which it is set up and lived out in real life.

Since the family is the primary living cell of the great

human community, it is evident that, in a world that is changing radically and with dizzying speed, the family, too, must feel the winds of change.

For example, if you transplant a typical rural family to the middle of an industrial city, you expose it to an inevitable crisis.

Since the family is the seed cell of humanity, it must always be analyzed with great respect, and we should hesitate before using the scalpel of criticism upon it. Yet to deny that it can ever change could aggravate the crisis and make the very institution of the family explode into little pieces.

As in the case of all the other human institutions which the changes in the world have placed in a state of crisis, we must approach the problem of the family with seriousness, courage, hope and a profound faith in the immutable human values which allow man to go on being a man in all circumstances and in his obviously human institutions, since only thus can these institutions also be divine.

Every change in the institution that is the basis of the human community must begin with the conviction and certainty of being able to free man from the chains that prevent him from fulfilling himself and being an image of the Creator.

Any other criterion of manifest or camouflaged selfishness would be logically reprehensible and dishonest.

The Lesson of Experience

A holy old priest once said to me: "If marriage were an unfailing formula for happiness, the whole world would be happy today. But unfortunately, it just isn't so."

Certainly, if we look at the facts dispassionately, we find that there are very few really happy marriages, ones in which the thermometer of love has continued to rise with the years; families in which the ideal of integration between parents and children has taken place; those without betrayals in fact or in desire; those which are confident enough to proclaim publicly the success of their love and in which parents and children are free of unhealthy complexes. And this is true about Catholic and non-Catholic marriages.

The harsh experience of my years in the apostolate forces me to confess that, among the many thousands of families whom I got to know intimately, the immense majority of couples were just "putting up" with each other. They were plants that were no longer growing; their love had ceased to blossom. Unfortunately, for these couples, everything that meant renewal, discovery and growth took place outside the home.

I could write volumes on the bitter confidences that I received from husbands and wives of all ages and classes. If I had to reduce my experiences to numbers, I would go so far as to say that, at most, two out of every thousand of the couples I knew were really growing in love and accomplishing that total integration of man and woman which leads to the joyful discovery of oneself and to the profound happiness of life revealed as the possibility of giving oneself to another to make him or her happy.

I am speaking here especially about Christian marriage, sanctified by a sacrament.

My sad experience is that even those marriages which, on the surface, seem exemplary and ideal can offer some bitter surprises to anyone who examines them closely.

And my experience is not unique, for it has been confirmed time and time again by hundreds of priests who work with married people. Even laymen themselves are beginning to admit this sad fact, which not even they can explain.

I do not deny that the ideal marriage may not even exist in this poor world of ours or that a couple's maturing in love is not a simple thing but often presupposes an effort that may last a whole lifetime. I am not forgetting that even the strongest and most complete loves are never exempt from all trial. Nor am I closing my eyes to the fact that men and women often fall very short of their ideals. Yet I think that the harsh experience of millions of families who do not succeed in attaining a minimum of deep, intimate sharing of life, of ever-growing love, forces us to be realistic and examine, dispassionately and objectively, the present institution of the family.

And this is precisely what makes many people think that there should be a change.

The Family of the Future

It would be ingenuous to try to foretell exactly what the family of the future will be like. In this, as in so many other problems of our times, we must proceed carefully in search of a solution. We are convinced that the family of tomorrow will certainly be very different from that of today; but we do not yet know how it will be different, partly because the form it will eventually take will depend upon the efforts made by the human community to solve the problems that face the family today.

We certainly can't expect angels to come down from heaven and give us a press conference about what the family of the year 2001 will be like. We are the ones who must begin to bring about the transformation. But God is present in our efforts, our sincere desire and our hope of giving a new face to the union of men and women in love.

But while we cannot offer a detailed picture of what the family of the future ought to be, we can begin with the obvious deficiencies we see in it today and go on to point out some things that must be changed if we wish to help relieve the crisis that is daily becoming graver.

As for myself, I should like to draw attention to some points as the beginning of a solution and as my personal contribution based on my experiences and the innumerable confidences I have received about a matter that I consider gravely urgent because it affects the core of man and the heart of the community.

Beyond the Contract

Until recently, the simple contract of marriage was considered sufficient foundation for the building of a family community. But today this is not accepted by theologians, moralists, psychologists or sociologists. From the human as well as the Christian point of view, a truly stable community of life cannot exist without a deep foundation of love.

When Christ said "What God has joined together, let no man put asunder," He was referring to a union that was made consciously in the name of God, whom Christians believe to be the God of love. The personal, mature, conscious, free, joyful and proven love between a man and a woman; a love that has been sealed with the guarantee of a sacrament which confers upon it the mysterious power of a love that symbolizes the love between Christ and His Church—such a love can be destroyed only by a grave failure to obey the imperious note of one's conscience. No sane, honest man can cause this destruction, because a free, mature love which has been grafted on to the Creator's own love belongs to God Himself and enters the mysterious category of the infinite, the definitive, the eternal.

But precisely for this reason, it is necessary to ask oneself whether or not a very large proportion of existing marriages were joined together by God and by deep love, or whether they are the result of sheer instinct, social imperatives, economic need or convenience, the force of custom or a thousand other imponderable factors which have nothing to do with a conscious, free and joyful choice.

Many couples get married, live together and "put up" with each other because of needs which are very different from love's urge for union with the loved one and for fulfilling itself in a fruitful and ever-new love. Consequently, such marriages are not formed in the name, and under the creative power, of the God of love.

In cases like these, we should have the courage to admit that they are not Christian marriages, and that the sacrament has never existed in them, because at no time were they even a pale image of Christ's love for His Church, that is, of that profound, unique love which embraces a man and a woman in all the aspects of their complex and almost divine personalities.

The First Necessity

I know that more than a few people will agree that many marriages are not really marriages at all because, from the beginning, they lacked the essential element of a free, personal and mature love. But even those who agree with me will object that very few would get married if they had to wait until they were morally certain of possessing such a love. Furthermore, experience shows that some of the marriages which apparently begin with this great love, later began to wither, leaving the couples prisoners of selfishness and emotional sterility.

This objection is a serious one and does not admit of an easy answer.

We all readily accept that a positive vocation is necessary for some modes of life, for example, the religious life, and that a lack of negative motives is not enough, whereas we light-heartedly believe that everybody has a vocation to marriage, and that it is sufficient to be male and female and be able to achieve the physical consummation of love in order to enter a lasting union, sealed with a sacrament. We can anticipate that perhaps all this will have to be changed.

I would not be greatly surprised if the Church became much more severe and began to demand guarantees of a vocation to marriage before granting admittance to the sacrament. The minimum requirement for this vocation would be a moral certainty that the man and woman would be able to attain serious integration with each other in the various fields of sexuality, psychology, ideological and religious affinity, etc. Because, while it is true that a great degree of affinity is not needed for free men simply to live together, and the mutual desire for brotherly exchange is sufficient, much more than this is necessary for the lifelong, complete sharing of one's life with that person whom one has selected as the ideal partner, to whom one will surrender the best of oneself in order to lay the foundations for an ideal community, the prototype of the great human community.

We shall not pause here to discuss the idea of a vocation to marriage. But there is one point which I think is fundamental in answering the objection mentioned above, a point that is the result of team-discussions which I had with some of those happy, exceptional couples who have realized their ideal fully and who are living out a love that continues to grow, which is new each day and which not even the greatest problems have been able to smother or diminish.

Those who have solved the problem of marriage have done it by sharing the conviction that a deep personal love can't exist between a man and woman if they have not solved beforehand the problem of universal love, that is, love for all mankind.

Only he who has opened himself up to a love without boundaries, who has succeeded in making all men, near and far, the object of his love; who has understood and acted upon the idea that his love should extend to everyone; only such a person is able to make the concrete choice of the one to whom he will offer, not only his love, which he will continue to give to each and every one, but also his very person, his body, his total and unfaltering collaboration, so that together, but not isolated from everybody else, they may undertake the fruitful adventure of their lives.

Those who lock themselves away from love of others under the pretext of giving "all their love" to one person, and those who have not bothered about opening their hearts up to universal love, are heading for disaster in their marriage because they are really offering their partners only a love that is very small indeed and incapable of growing.

If someone has chosen the partner with whom he wishes to express this universal love in tangible form, and if he demands that this partner renounce universal love, not only for humanity in general but also for the concrete individuals who make up that humanity, he is radically denying the dynamic of love.

Love is God's great gift to man, so great that He made man free in order that he might be able to love; and He gives it to us so that it might be universal and grow by being shared. Christ's great commandment was not "Love the one whom you have chosen to form a perfect, definitive community with you," but rather "Love one another!" Love for a person whom I can call "My love!" is only a choice within universal love.

When I say "universal love," I do not mean an intellectual emotion, an abstract love that has no real object. Instead, it is a concrete, real love, the love of true friendship, of collaboration in the process of history and in the expansion of family community.

This is the sense in which people are beginning to speak about "marriage communities."

Difficult? Of course it is! But it is completely Christian and, in my experience, the only solution to the problems of thousands of couples who, by dint of protecting themselves against every love that does not begin and end in themselves, and by exalting the nature of their love, have ended up by converting that love into an idol that finally crumbles into dust between their fingers.

We have been afraid to enlarge the concept of married

love, even in the strictest Christian sense, lest we make it too easy; and we really have not understood that what we were avoiding was the real difficulty entailed by a unique love incarnated in a universal love. We have also said that this is impossible, so that we could cover up our selfishness and avoid the difficulty of struggling and searching.

But Christian love is universal, and those who unite in marriage are not exempt from this universal dimension of love, for it is a love that does not take anything from the definitive and total surrender of oneself, because it must belong to everyone although our persons and our lives may have been freely given over to only one partner.

It is not easy to say this, but those who have even the least understanding of true universal Christian love will be able to see that this is very far from "free love," that crude caricature that is really neither love nor free, neither universal nor unique, but is only selfishness and prostitution. Here we can very aptly quote the words of Christ: "He who has ears to hear, let him hear!"

Personal Freedom in Marriage

If this universal love is to be possible even in marriage, and if it is to be the fountain that nourishes and keeps fresh the personal and definitive love between the man and the woman, there must obviously be a profound transformation in the life-style and the very psychology of the family. It is essential to ensure the necessary margin of personal freedom for both spouses.

It is not enough to say that those who are joined in marriage must not shut themselves up in their love but should open out to others; it is not enough to hold theoretically that the husband and wife must not renounce universal love. This universal love must be attainable in practice and must be possible, not only for the husband, but also for the wife.

And this is a difficult matter which must be thrashed out

by the man and woman together.

Up to the present, the man has been favored by social structures that were built along exclusively masculine lines, and he has thus obtained quite a large margin of freedom outside the family that has permitted him, at the least, to keep up contact with other men in his work, in his social life, in sports, etc.

But normally the result of all this is not the exercise of that universal love about which we have been speaking. Instead, the man considers this freedom as a right, and he justifies it like this: "A fellow can't be stuck in the house all day! If I don't socialize my work will suffer. I need my friends to widen my professional contacts." And he finds it even easier to prove that he needs a secretary or a nurse or whoever else is "useful" in his work.

If, now and then, his wife complains that he is too free and independent, he uses his simplest and most unanswerable argument: "After all, I'm a *man*!"

But even the margin of freedom which man has created for himself within marriage, often by sacrificing his wife's deepest feelings, is more a victory than a conquest, because the wife just puts up with it, saying: "If I get mad at him, I'll see even less of him!"

This is not a freedom which the wife has given her husband consciously and generously so that he may go on developing himself by remaining in contact with his friends, so that he may fulfil himself better, and so that the "unique" love which he gives her may be ever newer and better, since the heart grows larger only by loving everyone. The wife does not give the husband this freedom; rather it is something that the huband claims as the masculine spoils of war.

And here both priests and psychologists could speak about the enormous tensions which this "victorious" freedom of the husbands—which, after all, is very limited and quite small—creates in the hearts of so many wives. Nevertheless, the fact is that the married man has a very real margin of freedom which allows him to extend the limits of his love and his life with his fellows. This is why the man generally remains more alive, younger, more active, more open to the realities of history and to world problems. Therefore the man is generally more politically-minded than the woman, and the woman is more inclined this way before marriage than she is afterwards.

The greatest tension arises from the fact that the wife does not possess this real margin of freedom which the husband has and which is often consciously denied her because of her function as "wife and mother."

We take it for granted that jealousy is typically feminine, whereas in reality most men are much more jealous than any woman, in spite of the fact that their margin of freedom is much greater. The man has no trouble in proving that his work requires him to broaden the field of his friendship and social relationships. But if his wife even thinks about taking a job outside the home, he raises all kinds of difficulties because he wants to spare her every temptation and danger, to keep her tied to the house and to remain exclusively his.

He justifies all this by pointing out the duties of motherhood, but he cannot quote any passage from the Gospel where Christ exempts the father from his responsibility of fatherhood. Nature itself has, in fact, provided that the woman can go on working almost up to the moment of giving birth. And nowhere is it written in the Gospel that it must always be the mother, and never the father, who has to get up and take care of the baby when it cries during the night. Some may say that it is a law of nature that the mother, and not the father, should be principally concerned about the protection of the newborn child. But if this is so, then we should be more consistent in following this law to its logical conclusions, as we shall see later.

Certainly if the man fulfils himself in his work, in his social contacts and in his exchange of ideas and opinions with them, then the woman should be given the same freedom to develop. And even motherhood should be subordinate to the woman's self-development, because if she does not first fulfil herself, does not first discover that she is truly human, and if she cannot continue to develop in all dimensions, then she will not be able to be a good mother.

To think otherwise would be to regard women more as objects than as human companions, more as servants than as indispensable partners in that union in which both partners become fully human and children of God.

As one wife said to me, "When we get married, we become housemaids who get no pay and no days off!" This many sound cynical, but it is not far from the truth.

The gravest consequence of the married woman's lack of freedom to fulfil herself as a human being, to work, to be something more than a mere housewife or nursemaid, is the imbalance that it inevitably creates in the social and psychological atmosphere of the family.

I have mentioned previously that only very few of the married couples I have known have succeeded in increasing their love over the years. And now I must confess that even fewer of these couples shared together in the whole intellectual and cultural contents, or even the mere surface details, of their lives and work.

It is frightening to see the loneliness and lack of dialogue in marriage as regards the husband's problems in his work, which is really what occupies his whole day.

And this is true at all levels of society.

When the engineer, the lawyer, the doctor, the electrician, the politician, the mailman or the plumber finishes his day's work and returns home, he doesn't speak to his wife about his work because, as he says, "She can't understand me"; or "It would only complicate things if she got mixed up in my work"; or "Why should I worry her with my problems?" etc. For her part, the wife says: "I don't even dare to ask him about his work. That's a whole world I've never been able to enter." And as one would expect, the wife will always want to talk about the same things—the children and the way they're doing in school; the bills; the phone calls she got; what Mrs. So-and-so next door said or did, etc. And even when the husband doesn't get angry and shout, "I have enough problems in work!" he will try to escape by turning on the television, burying himself in the newspaper or playing with the children.

Stated as simply as this, the problem may seem childish, but it really is a serious one.

A short while ago, the wife of a politician said to me, "My last free act was to say 'Yes' at the altar, and since then I have been living like a prisoner, locked up in my golden cage." And she added, "The appalling thing is that I married my husband because I admired his intelligence, his work and his ideas. And now we practically never speak about what he's doing. I have to depend upon his friends to tell me about his work. I myself have given up all intellectual effort because I never get a chance to talk to him about such things, and I spend my life in the kitchen and with the children."

Perhaps men don't realize that, when they get married, they often acquire more freedom than before, because they are no longer accountable to their parents, they have someone to look after their household and worry about the smaller details of daily living; they have someone whom they can "order" to do things for them. But things are quite different for the woman in the present structure of marriage; when she gets married, her freedom is so curtailed that it practically disappears.

That is why so many wives—many more than one would suppose—pine for the freedom of their youth. At least then they could study, work, go out with their friends, travel and enjoy a certain amount of economic independence.

Lack of liberty prevents the wife from working, widening her interests and continuing her education in the broad sense of the term. And this in turn makes it virtually impossible for her to carry on a meaningful conversation with her husband about his work, the type of conversation he has every day with the women he works with. As a result of this lack of dialogue, the wife gets lonely and becomes wrapped up in the children when they are small and in the grandchildren when they begin to appear; or, at best, she has a few women friends or neighbors who are in the same boat and who meet to console each other.

I've heard it said that this is the way things must be, but I think all this is a grave injustice to the woman, a relic of slavery and the root cause of the present day crises in the family and the increasing number of broken homes.

Equality of rights as regards freedom, work and the need to go on growing as a person is urgent if we are to have a better future for the institution of marriage and perhaps even if the institution is to survive.

Some young people angrily refuse to accept what they call the "closed circle" of marriage, that is to say, binding oneself forever to the same person. At times, this attitude may be the result of unbridled selfishness or an appallingly superficial idea of love. But it may also be the intuition which the new generation has into the fact that man and wife need that universal love which does not contradict their love for each other. Many of the new generation feel that, to reach self-fulfilment, a man, as it were, needs every woman, and a woman every man; that there is no human being who does not enrich another; and that marriage does not compel the spouses to love only one another but is instead the happiness of sharing this universal love with only one person in a unique way; and that this universal love is not libertinism but is a transparently Christian love, a generous love that is real and concrete.

What Shall We Do With the Children?

I know quite well that it is not easy to put these principles into practice in a society and culture that are completely "masculine" products.

Even those women who are most receptive to this new approach to marriage are fully aware of the practical difficulties presented by the proposed changes, and they want to know: "What shall we do with the children? How can I go to work or study when I have three or four small children to take care of and no help in the home? Who's going to look after the house and my husband?"

Certainly, if we put it like that, the problem is insoluble.

But if we want to save the family as a stable, definitive institution for the future that is pressing upon us, we must start from other premises and have the courage to approach the problem from other angles, laying aside old prejudices and freeing ourselves of ancestral taboos and undue sentimentality.

Although many people may be scandalized when I say it, I think that our super-technical world still has much to learn about children from Mother Nature.

The wise men of all ages have found that the life-style of the animals was a good school in which to learn how to conduct human society, not a perfect school by any means, but one which they could imitate in its basic and essential values.

And I think that, as regards the father-son relationship, we have not perfected nature but rather prostituted it. In the animal kingdom, the fathers are more generous with their sons than we are with ours, giving them as soon as possible the freedom that they need to be themselves. What they do by instinct, we should do out of conviction and generosity.

In the animal kingdom, the offspring do not remain close to their parents for a long time and certainly not long enough to be formed into their image and likeness. As soon as possible, the young animals break away to begin their personal adventure with all its risks but also with all its possibilities for self-development.

There are human parents who would like to keep their sons close to them until they get married and, if possible, even afterwards; who want their sons to be like themselves, not only in appearance, but also even in their actions and the smallest detail of their political opinions.

In our civilization, because of the father's absence from the home, the rearing of the sons is usually left to the mother. Hence the lack of manliness in our new generation, which has been formed almost exclusively by women; and hence, too, the alarming increase in the number of Oedipus complexes.

It is not so much that the girls of today are becoming masculine but rather that the young men are losing their manliness through lack of contact with their fathers and through over-protectiveness on the part of their mothers, who, in the absence of the fathers, pour out all their love on the sons.

According to an ethnologist of my acquaintance, the problems of effeminate youths or Oedipus complexes does not exist in those primitive tribes in which the woman goes out working while the man stays at home, smoking his pipe and chatting with the other men or else goes hunting with his sons. Indeed, if anything, the young men of these tribes suffer from an excess of manliness.

In the family of the future, the father will have to have the courage to allow the sons to begin as soon as possible to develop their own characteristics and personalities, since the Creator Himself has decreed that there should be no two human beings exactly alike.

If this is to come about, it is important that the sons begin to work and earn their living as soon as possible. They will have to work and study at the same time; they will have to be able to stand on their own feet, not when the parents finally get around to allowing it, but when the sons can do so naturally.

By saying this, we do not wish to minimize in the least the indispensable role of the parents in the rearing of the children: but we do wish to make a plea for an upbringing that will not smother the children's personalities and will allow them to be themselves as soon as possible. Parents themselves should be the very ones who should seek out the best ways to accelerate this process.

The size of the family, too, should be in accordance with the maturity of the spouses' relationship with each other. It is true that married love is essentially fruitful and tends to multiply itself; but it is also true, and becoming clearer every day, that the important thing is not the number of children but that each human being who comes into the world should be as free and as much a child of God as possible. Therefore, since a margin of freedom is necessary for both spouses if they are to mature, it would be as erroneous and unjust to compromise this maturation by having too large a family as it would be to limit the family from purely selfish motives.

It is mere sentimentality to object that the woman has been created for motherhood and that if she wants a large family, she should not deny herself even to promote greater harmony and maturity in the family. We are inclined to be irrational on this point because, while we are afraid to imitate the animals literally in the freedom which they give their offspring, we have no hesitation in confining motherhood to its purely instinctive and natural role.

While the husbands will have to control and "humanize"

their sexual instinct for various reasons, since men ought to be master over all their instincts and channel them for the benefit of man himself, similarly the wives will have to regulate and "humanize" their maternal instinct, both in the number of their children as well as in their tendency to keep the children tied to their apron-strings as long as possible.

In these matters, it is always a question of men and women, husbands and wives, working together to free mankind, and both men and women can be free only if they are allowed to acquire an authentically human freedom. If this freedom is really human, it will be divine also, even if those who possess it do not advert to the fact.

I would go so far as to say that only the married couple that has achieved personal integration and maturity in love has the right to bring a new being into the world. This is so because it is useless to speak about rearing children in a marriage in which a free, mature and human encounter has not taken place. If children cannot see in their parents that the union of a man and a woman is a joyful encounter of love which becomes more perfect each day, they will always be burdened with scepticism and complexes.

In my opinion, a marriage in which the husband hides himself in his work or his friends, and the wife in her children, is already a broken home which resembles simple instinctive nature more than it does a human, Christian society. And I ask myself if couples like this even have the right to procreate.

Therefore, I really think that, faced as we are with the hard reality of the facts, we cannot afford to throw stones at those who dare to question the present institution of marriage. Instead, we who believe firmly in the legitimacy and necessity of marriage and its possibility of sharing in the mystery of God's own love should have the courage to ask ourselves some pointed questions that could be the beginning of the changes needed for the family of the future.

In this chapter, we have tried to ask some of these key questions without worrying too much about drawing a clear picture of what we believe the family of the future will be like. There are no ready-made solutions, and we have to provide answers every day by working together in an honest community effort. We must strive to give a new face to that truth which the Christian cannot reject without degrading human dignity itself, that is to say, the possibility of total and final integration between a man and a woman in order to form a perfect community of married love within the wider circle of a sincere universal love.

Being Truly Human

Finally, we must acknowledge that if we do not first face the problem of the individual, there is no possibility of a renewal in family life or of creating a better model for the family, more human and more free. Before all else, the individual human being, man or woman, must discover his infinite existence in time, his personal, concrete reality; he must become aware of his dignity as a free being, created for happiness through love of his fellowmen; he must be convinced that man and woman are already perfect beings in themselves, made in the image and likeness of God, and that they are not dependent on the "man-woman" union in order to be fully human and children of God. Each individual is perfect in himself; he is almost a God, as the Bible says.

Only by starting with this conviction can we begin to solve the problem, not of the "self-fulfilment," but of the "integration," of the man and the woman in a personal community of love.

In the Bible, when God created woman, he said, "It is not good for man to be alone." But He did not say that man would not be complete as an individual being without woman, or woman without man. It is not a question of two halves of the same apple, or two pieces of the one machine, but of two complete persons, two perfect realities, two free, responsible beings, each with its own name, its own richness; two different but not incomplete persons.

Man and woman are two human and almost divine beings whom the Creator has shaped for a personal, human encounter in love, with a capacity for spiritual and bodily dialogue, and with a need for forming a personal community for the benefit of the universal community.

When God said: "It is not good . . ." He was not speaking about something that was necessary for man but only good and advantageous for him, something to combat man's original solitude, a solitude that is broken especially by the integration of man and woman at all levels of life.